WEEKEND MAKES

ENGLISH PAPER PIECING

25 QUICK AND EASY PROJECTS TO MAKE

WEEKEND MAKES

ENGLISH PAPER PIECING

25 QUICK AND EASY PROJECTS TO MAKE

JANET GODDARD AND JEMIMA SCHLEE

First published 2022 by
Guild of Master Craftsman Publications Ltd
Castle Place, 166 High Street, Lewes,
East Sussex, BN7 1XU

ISBN 978 1 78494 643 2

Managing Art Editor: Darren Brant
Art Editor: Jennifer Stephens
Editor: Wendy Hobson
Photography: Sian Irvine
Stylist: Sian Irvine

Colour origination by GMC Reprographics
Printed and bound in China

CONTENTS

INTRODUCTION

Welcome to *Weekend Makes: English Paper Piecing*, featuring 25 bright and modern projects to make for yourself, your home or to give as gifts.

I think of English paper piecing (EPP) as a bit like a jigsaw puzzle, except with fabric! You use paper templates that fit together just like a puzzle. You wrap fabric around each template and then hand stitch the shapes together to create a design. The paper template shapes ensure that the blocks are accurate and they make it easy to piece angles together. Once sewn, remove the papers and you have a beautifully pieced patchwork, which can be used to create cushions, pouches, coasters, bags and a variety of other projects.

The great thing about English paper piecing is that it requires very little equipment: a needle, some pins, a pair of scissors, paper templates and some fabric scraps and you are off. It's portable, too, which is a huge bonus in this busy world. It's great when you are commuting or on the move as it takes up very little space and the project can be slipped into a small bag to keep it all together and easily carried around.

It is also totally relaxing. To snatch a half hour here and there and absorb yourself in some EPP is a mindful and calming experience.

In this book, each project starts by creating a piece of EPP, then the patchwork can be stitched into a small item. Some of the items can be stitched by hand, but if you wish to speed up the process, many can be completed on a sewing machine. They are all marked either 'Beginner' or 'Confident' so you can choose an easy project or something a bit more challenging involving a few extra techniques. They may take a little longer, but you can easily fit a project into a weekend.

We start with a section on the techniques involved. It explains how to make and use templates, details each stage of the EPP process and gives guidance on fabric selection and materials. Once you are familiar with the process it's time to begin a project – and there are 25 imaginative and attractive options to choose from!

Janet Goddard.

HOW ENGLISH PAPER PIECING BEGAN

English paper piecing is a historical patchwork technique that can be traced back to the 1700s. The earliest hexagon template that quilt researchers have found was made in England in 1770, while the oldest known paper-pieced quilt top in the UK is the 1718 silk patchwork coverlet, which can be found in the Quilters' Guild Collection.

EPP involves using scraps of fabric, basted around paper templates, usually hexagonal in shape, and then sewn together to create beautiful patterns. Since paper used to be a luxury, paper-pieced quilts were generally made in wealthy households. Even so, the templates were often cut out from old letters, newspapers, household bills and periodicals. As these papers were frequently left in the quilts (for an extra layer of warmth), they have been a great help in enabling historians to accurately date old quilts.

The first known published hexagon pattern appeared in *Godey's Lady's Book* in 1835; it contained complete instructions for the paper-piecing construction technique. By that time, using hexagons for EPP had become one of the most popular patterns and styles in England and the United States, and was often known as mosaic or honeycomb patchwork.

The popularity of different patterns has changed over the years, not least as a reaction to austerity. When times are hard, every last scrap has to be put to work, and patchwork is a great way to utilize scarce pieces of fabric. This was clearly demonstrated in the difficult post-war and Depression years of the 1920s and 1930s. At that time, the pattern called Grandmother's Flower Garden became a very popular style of piecing. The design is a rosette made from seven hexagons which grows from the middle outwards. Each rosette is surrounded by a plain fabric, linking the rosettes together. The pattern remains popular today, providing a wonderful connection to quilters of the past.

Now, several strands of the modern zeitgeist are coming together to encourage a resurgence of interest in this delightful craft: the focus on upcycling and avoiding waste; busy lifestyles with time snatched for creative crafts; people on the move wanting portable entertainment; and the modern need for simple ways to destress and switch off from the constant hum of high technology all around us.

BASIC TECHNIQUES

TEMPLATES

All English paper piecing needs templates.
Historically, templates were made from
whatever paper was to hand, including old
letters, circulars, magazines and paper packaging
– and you can still re-use in this way – although
today there are so many more options available.

How you make the templates and paper shapes
is a personal preference but the alternatives
have been described below. Full-size templates
for all the projects can be found at the back
of the book (pages 138–141) and these can be
used in the following ways.

Tip
You will need to make different shapes
of template for your projects. Don't
be confused by the terms 'five-point
diamond' or 'six-point dianond'. They
simply mean the number of diamonds
that will fit together in a circle to make
a star pattern.

Tracing

Use tracing paper to transfer the template onto
cardboard or clear plastic. Carefully cut out the
template, ensuring that accuracy is maintained.
Use the template to make the paper shapes
for the patchwork project by tracing around
the template, creating the number of paper
shapes needed. The shapes can be traced onto
scrap paper, old magazine pages or plain white
photocopy paper. This method is a really good
option for re-using what is to hand.

Photocopying

Photocopy the templates provided in the section
at the back of the book. If you are using this
method, do double check the accuracy of the
shapes once copied as sometimes the printer
or photocopier can slightly distort images.
Alternatively there are many websites that
offer free downloadable templates and you may
wish to check these out. If you choose to use
these, again, do check their accuracy against the
templates at the back of the book to ensure that
these are the same size as those needed.

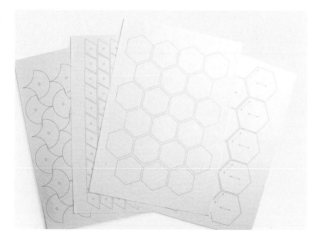

Freezer paper

Freezer paper can be used to make the shapes. This paper is traditionally used for wrapping food but is often used for various types of patchwork and can be purchased in a roll from quilt shops. One side of the paper has a slight plastic coating so when it is heated it sticks the paper to the fabric. The shapes are used in the usual way for EPP, although they are stuck lightly to the fabric. When you have finished piecing, the papers can be removed by peeling them away from the fabric.

Ready-cut paper templates

This final method is my go-to option. I usually buy pre-cut template shapes, which are widely available both in shops and online and come in packs containing single or multiple shapes in a variety of sizes. I especially like the weight of the papers as they are usually thicker than standard paper but not as thick as card, and you always know that the shapes are completely accurate as they have been machine cut. If you are purchasing pre-cut shapes, do ensure that the sizes of the shapes match those of the chosen project. A standard measurement for each side of a hexagon for paper piecing is usually 2in (5cm).

Acrylic, plastic and metal templates

Ready-made acrylic, plastic and metal templates are widely available and can be traced around to create the paper shapes. Acrylic templates are also great for fussy cutting (page 17) motifs and designs from fabric. They often come with the seam allowance included.

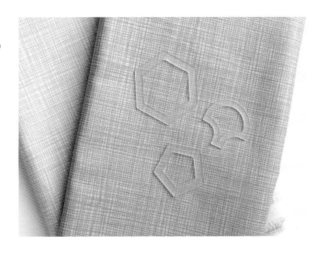

FABRICS AND THREAD

FABRICS

One of the nicest parts of starting a new project is being able to choose the fabrics.

The fabrics chosen for each project in this book have been selected to take into account the purpose of each item and how much use it will have. I use fabric that is 100 per cent cotton, although you can use other similar fabrics if you prefer. When selecting a number of different fabrics, however, it is important that they are all of a similar weight. The fabric also needs to be thin enough to wrap around the shapes but thick enough to hold its shape. Fabric scraps can be used for many of the projects and these can be coordinated by colour or used randomly.

The scale of the print on the fabric used is an important factor in EPP because if the shapes are small, a smaller fabric print is more effective and if the shapes are larger, a bigger scale print is perfect.

The patterns chosen for these projects are bright, modern and with a variety of designs. Each project details the fabric colour and print that has been used but you can substitute your own fabric choices to suit.

The fabric allowances in the patterns are for fabric that is approximately 42in (107cm) wide from selvedge to selvedge. I always cut the selvedge off the fabric before beginning a project and I rarely pre-wash fabrics, but this is a personal choice. The fabric allowances in each pattern allow for 2–3in (5–7.6cm) extra, so if a small mistake is made you shouldn't run out of fabric. However, do try to be as careful as possible.

THREAD AND OTHER NOTIONS

If you choose to tack or baste your EPP shapes to the fabric, you can use any type of thread. I always think that tacking the papers to the fabric is a good opportunity to use up ends of thread reels that you may have sitting around, although I do try to use a thread colour that contrasts significantly with the fabric so that it is highly visible when the time comes to remove the tacking.

To stitch the shapes together I use a high-quality 50-weight thread in a colour that matches the fabrics being used. Where it is not possible to match the thread precisely as there are so many contrasting fabrics being used, I tend to use a neutral colour such as a soft grey or beige thread that blends well with multi colours.

Everything you need in the way of fastenings – such as zips, buttons, ribbons and so on – is listed at the top of each project.

MEASUREMENTS

Imperial standard measurements have been used throughout the patterns, but the metric measurements have been included as well. It is best to use either imperial or metric, rather than mixing the two together.

All the cutting instructions for the projects include a ¼in (0.65cm) seam allowance unless otherwise specified.

Especially when you begin to branch out and use patterns from different sources, always check whether the seam allowances have been included in the pattern templates and, if so, how much.

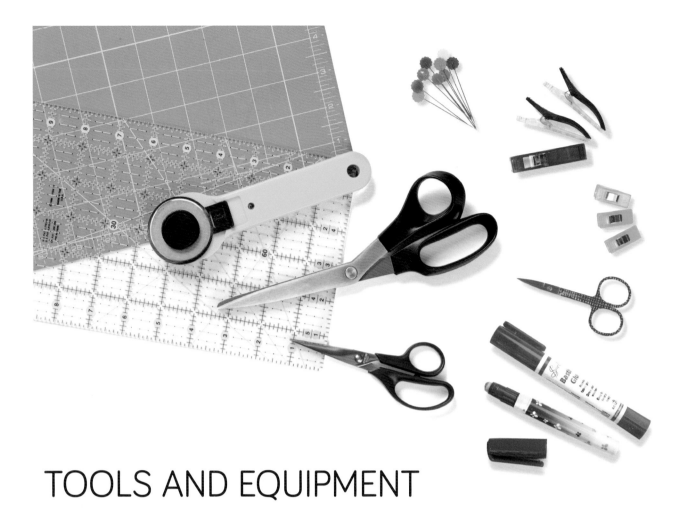

TOOLS AND EQUIPMENT

Good-quality basic equipment is needed to make these projects. All you really need are needles, pins, scissors and an iron and ironing board.

Scissors: A good, sharp pair of dressmaking scissors is essential for cutting fabric. A medium-size pair is useful for cutting off corners and trimming, while a small pair is handy for snipping threads. Paper scissors are also needed for cutting out the templates.

Pins: I use fine, flat flowerhead pins or glass-headed pins as they help to keep the fabric flat, but any type of pins will do.

Needles: For EPP, a fine, sharp hand-sewing needle is important. These come in a variety of sizes and with different-sized eyes. You may also need a quilting needle.

Thimble: Everyone holds a needle slightly differently so everyone needs a different solution for protecting their fingers. Thimbles come in myriad shapes and sizes, some metal, some plastic or silicone. Some people like to wear a thimble on the index finger, holding the fabric on the top of the work, while others like to wear a thimble on a finger underneath the project – sometimes people wear both. My personal choice is a silicone thimble with a metal top as I like the way the thimble stays securely on my finger while the metal is good for pushing the needle through the fabric.

Quilting ruler: These come in many shapes and sizes, are marked in inches or centimetres and are usually made of tough acrylic. I personally find the rulers with yellow markings the easiest to see on fabric but this is a personal choice.

Fabric markers: There are many fabric markers available but any marker should be easy to use, easy to see and simple to remove after you have finished sewing. Markers are used to mark measurements for cutting or stitching and also quilting lines or patterns. Several different coloured markers are needed in order to contrast with both light and dark fabrics. White and silver markers, water-erasable pens and chalk markers are all useful.

Seam ripper: This is often called a 'quick unpick' and usually comes as a tool with the sewing machine. Hugely useful for removing tacking (basting) stitches or unpicking the odd mistake we all make now and then, it can also be used to unpick seams.

Glue stick: A glue stick or glue pen can be used to temporarily glue the paper templates to the fabric instead of pinning and tacking. Once the papers are removed, the light residue of glue left on the fabric can be washed away.

Sewing machine: Once the EPP has been hand stitched, it is a good idea to finish making the project on the sewing machine. The sewing machine really only needs to be able to stitch forwards and backwards and doesn't need a whole lot of fancy stitches, although a zigzag stitch can be handy for neatening seams. This usually comes as a standard feature on most modern machines.

It is important that your machine is cared for and is cleaned and serviced regularly to keep it working well. A little oil applied according to the manufacturer's instructions should help to keep everything in good order. Changing the needle regularly also helps with the quality of stitching, so I usually change the needle on the machine every time I begin a new project.

The machine feet used the most are the general machine foot, the ¼in (0.65cm) patchwork foot – which is excellent for maintaining ¼in (0.65cm) wide seams – and the zipper foot. If you are quilting, you may need a walking foot (page 23).

Clips: When pins aren't quite enough, little plastic clips are great for holding multiple layers of fabric together for tasks like hand stitching a binding to a project or top stitching around the top of a bag. Think mini clothes pegs but better because they are designed specifically for the job! They can be removed easily as you stitch.

Iron and ironing board: The iron is an essential tool in EPP. A press with a dry iron at each stage is all that is needed and the use of a good-quality iron does make a difference to the finished product. The ironing surface needs to be firm and clean.

Rotary cutter and cutting mat (optional): A rotary cutter is a cutting instrument with a round-wheeled blade that is used with an acrylic ruler and a self-healing cutting mat. A good-quality rotary cutter should have a protective safety shield on it that can be pushed on and off. It is important to train yourself to make sure that the safety cover is always on the blade every time the cutter is put down. Blades are sharp and can cut through up to eight layers of fabric at a time and so can do a lot of damage to hands if not kept safe. Replace the blades when they start to become blunt.

A rotary cutting mat is a self-healing mat designed to be used with a rotary cutter. Mats come with grid markings on them which can be used with the ruler for accurate cutting. If you are purchasing a mat for the first time buy the largest you can afford. A 24 × 36in (61 × 91cm) mat is a good investment.

BASIC EPP TECHNIQUES

CUTTING THE FABRICS

The fabric shapes for your project can be cut in several ways depending on the number and variety of shapes to be cut. Choose the method that works best for you.

For all the methods, you can use dressmaking scissors or a rotary cutter with a quilting ruler and a mat.

Strip cutting

Perfect for cutting multiple shapes from the same fabric as it is very economical. To determine how wide to cut the fabric strips, measure the width of your paper template and add ¾in (1.9cm) to this measurement. Cut your fabric into long strips of this width and then pin your paper templates to the wrong side of the fabric strip, leaving a ¾in (1.9cm) space between each shape. Cut the shapes apart.

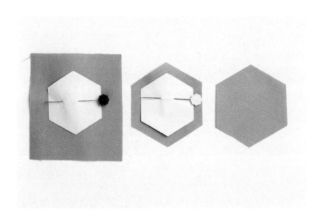

Single shape cutting

This involves placing the paper template on the wrong side of the fabric, pinning it in place and then cutting around the shape leaving a ⅜in (1cm) seam allowance of fabric around the shape on all sides. This is a great method for small projects or those that have a number of different shapes. It is also perfect when working with small scraps of fabric.

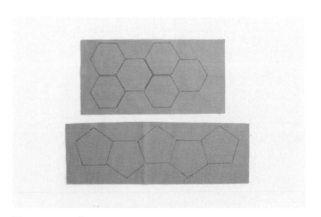

Tracing and cutting

This is also a good method for cutting fabric shapes in larger quantities. Firstly make a cardboard or plastic template of the shape required, ensuring that you add the ⅜in (1cm) seam allowance to each edge. Trace around the cardboard or plastic shape onto the reverse of your fabric with a marking pen or pencil. The shapes can be rotated and butted up to each other to make the most efficient use of the fabric. Ready-made acrylic, plastic and metal templates can be used for this method.

Fussy cutting

A wonderful technique that showcases a design feature or specific motif in the fabric, it uses an acrylic or a cardboard template with the middle cut away, creating a window. To fussy cut the fabrics, take your template and move it around on the right side of the fabric until you have your chosen motif in the middle of the window. Draw around the template and then cut out the fabric shape.

ROTARY CUTTING

A rotary cutter is particularly useful for cutting regular shapes. If you are new to using a rotary cutter it is worth spending some time practising on scrap fabric, as accuracy does improve with practice.

It is easier to stand and cut rather than sit when using a cutter, and a kitchen work surface is usually at an appropriate height. Iron the fabric to remove any wrinkles, then place the fabric on a self-healing mat. To cut safely, always hold

the cutter firmly in your hand at a 45-degree angle and place your other hand flat on the ruler with the fingers slightly opened, making sure that your fingers are away from the edge of the ruler. Flip the safety cover off the cutter and place the blade next to the ruler. Starting at the bottom of the fabric, begin to cut away from yourself until you have cut past the end of the fabric. Close the safety cover on the cutter before putting it down.

To cut off the selvedge from a piece of fabric, fold the fabric selvedge to selvedge, then fold in half again so you have four layers of selvedge together. You may be able to fold again if the fabric is not too thick. Ensure that all the layers are smooth. Place the ruler firmly on top of the fabric and cut the selvedge from the fabric, tidying up any uneven edges.

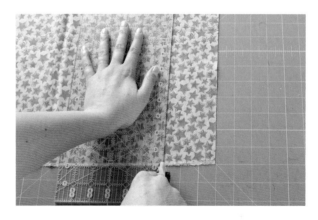

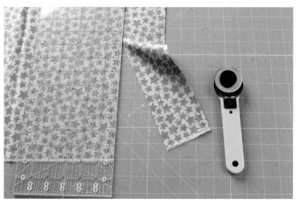

Strip cutting

To cut strips of fabric from which further shapes can be cut, align the even horizontal edge of the fabric with the first vertical measurement on the cutting board.

Place the ruler on top so that the measurement you wish to cut is in line with the edge of the fabric, for example if you wish to cut a 2in (5cm) strip, the 2in (5cm) marking of the ruler will be level with the cut edge of the fabric. Line up the cutter with the ruler and cut away from yourself.

Cutting shapes

If you wish to cut squares, place the strip on the cutting board horizontally and then, using the ruler vertically, measure the same width as the strip, keeping a ruler line on the long edge of the strip, ensuring that a right angle is maintained and that you are cross cutting the strip into squares. Rectangles can be cut in a similar manner.

Cutting right-angle triangles

To cut right-angled triangles, cut squares as described above, then cut the squares in half on the diagonal from corner to corner. Make sure that you hold the ruler firmly when cutting on the diagonal as it is easy to wobble and then the triangles will not be consistent in size.

PREPARING THE SHAPES

Once you have cut out your fabrics and paper templates you are ready to tack (baste) the papers to the fabric using thread or a fabric glue stick. Tacking has an important job to do as it holds the wrapped fabric around the shapes on a temporary basis until the patchwork is stitched together. Tacking stitches can be large and are best stitched in a thread that contrasts with the fabric being used.

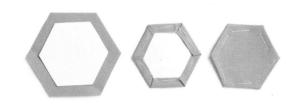

For large shapes

For shapes where the sides are 1in (2.5cm) or larger, pin the template to the wrong side of the fabric shape, ensuring that it is in the middle. The tacking stitches will go through the paper and the fabric. Working your way around the shape, fold over the seam allowance and stitch this down, working through both the paper and fabric, ensuring that where you have a corner or point, the folded fabric is securely tacked down.

For small shapes

For smaller shapes where the sides are less than 1in (2.5cm), pin the paper template to the wrong side of the fabric shape, ensuring that it is in the middle. As the shapes are so small the tacking stitch does not need to go through both the paper and the fabric but the stitches can simply be stitched through the seam allowance. Make a knot on the end of a thread. Fold the first edge of the fabric over the paper and take one stitch through the seam allowance. Working your way around the shape, fold the seam allowance over the paper, take a back stitch at each corner or point where the fabrics overlap, stitching only through the fabric. Repeat around all the corners. Secure your thread with a couple of backstitches. You are aiming to achieve a nice, crisp fold around all edges.

To glue baste shapes

The projects suggest tacking (basting) as this is the most popular method, but glue basting shapes is a more modern technique for securing the paper templates to the fabric. Place the paper template on the wrong side of the fabric shape. Run a fabric glue stick along one edge of the template and fold the fabric on to the glued edge. Continue in this way, one edge at a time, all around the shape. Avoid getting glue on the actual fold, otherwise it will be difficult to sew.

STITCHING THE SHAPES TOGETHER

Once the fabrics have been tacked or glued to the shapes, it is time to stitch the shapes together. If you can, it gives a better finish if you match the thread to the fabrics so that the stitches sink into the fabric and are not visible. However, this is not always possible if you are stitching shapes together that are very different colours. If this occurs, I always use a neutral colour thread such as a grey or beige.

Whip stitch

The stitch used to stitch the shapes together is a whip stitch, sometimes known as an overcast stitch. Basically it stitches over and over the folded edges. A good whip stitch should be small and even with the stitches close together. When you look at the shapes you have joined together, the stitches should be invisible on the right side of the fabric.

To whip stitch the shapes together, take two shapes and align the edges with right sides together. The edges should be exactly the same length. Knot the thread and take a small stitch into the seam allowance. Bring the needle out on one edge of the shapes that are to be stitched together, pass the needle through the fold of both fabric shapes, capturing just a few threads from each fabric, and then pull the thread through. You should not be stitching into the paper template but just the folded fabric. Repeat, stitching over and over the folded edges. Please note that in the middle photo I have used a contrasting thread for clarity.

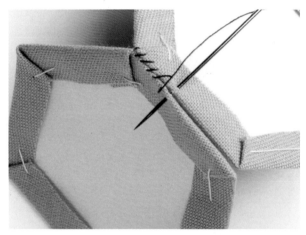

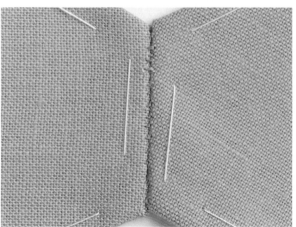

REMOVING THE TEMPLATE PAPERS

It is a good idea to keep the template papers in place until you are ready to stitch the patchwork into a project. It helps with stability.

Once the shapes have been stitched together, I always like to give the patchwork a good press before removing the papers. I think it helps to set the seams and stabilize the shapes before they are stitched into a project. As the papers are still intact, you need to be careful when using the iron and just press lightly. When to remove the papers depends on whether they were tacked (basted) or glued to the fabrics.

To remove the papers from large shapes

With the larger shapes you will have stitched through both the paper and the fabric so the tacking stitches will need to come out first. Carefully using a seam ripper, gently pull out the tacking stitches. When all the stitches have been removed, the papers will pop out.

To remove the papers from small shapes

As you have tacked the seam allowances by only stitching through the fabrics, you can leave the tacking in place, as it won't be seen on the front of the patchwork, and simply remove the papers by slipping your finger under the seam allowance and pulling out the paper.

To remove the papers from glue basted shapes

Using your finger, gently ease the fabric seam allowance away from the papers without fraying the fabric. Once you have done this, the papers can be removed.

If you remove the template papers carefully from your projects they will be able to be re-used again and again.

USING THE EPP PATCHWORK IN A PROJECT

You can use your EPP patchwork in two different ways. You can use the panel of EPP whole just as you would for a piece of patchwork by stitching it to other pieces of fabric or you can appliqué the finished piece of EPP to fabric and make it into a finished item.

Hand appliqué using hemming stitch

To appliqué the EPP by hand to the fabric, ensure that you have removed all the papers, then pin the patchwork to the fabric and, using a small hemming stitch, stitch the EPP to the fabric by stitching along the outer edge of the EPP.

Hemming stitch

To do a hemming stitch, take a small stitch into the background fabric and then a small stitch into the folded edge of the shape. Pull the thread securely.

Machine appliqué

To appliqué the EPP by machine to the fabric, ensure that all of the papers are removed, pin the patchwork to the fabric and, using a straight stitch on the sewing machine, stitch along the outer folded edge of the patchwork ⅛in (0.32cm) away from the folded edge.

CUTTING EPP TO FIT

For many projects you need a square or a rectangle of EPP to stitch in between other fabrics. Because of the tessellated nature of EPP, there are often edges where half shapes stick out. It is okay to trim these off in line with the other shapes to achieve the straight edge that you need. To do this you can draw a horizontal or vertical line with a marking pen or pencil and a ruler and then cut along the line with scissors or a rotary cutter and mat.

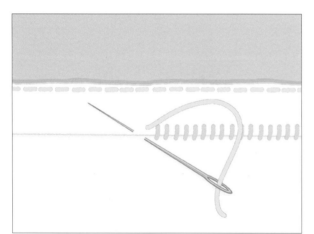

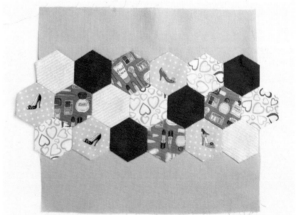

TECHNIQUES FOR FINISHING YOUR PROJECTS

Some of the projects require simple hand or machine finishing. These have been kept to the minimum but do give the projects a nice finish.

QUILTING

Some of the projects have been hand or machine quilted with simple straight or diagonal lines to hold the wadding (batting) to the fabric and/or to add texture. Using the machine's walking foot helps make quilting easier as the layers are fed through the machine evenly. If you do not have a walking foot you can use an ordinary presser foot, but make sure to reduce both the thread tension and foot pressure on the machine to prevent the layers from puckering. It can help to make a sample square of scrap fabric and wadding (batting) to test the settings before you start. I use the same thread in the top and bobbin of my machine, and use a 40-weight thread in a colour that complements the fabrics. The thread is strong, but fine enough to sink into the quilt layers to create texture. For hand quilting, I use a neat running stitch.

If you wish to quilt in straight vertical lines, use a fabric marking pencil to draw a line from top to bottom down the middle of the project. Stitch the first line of quilting on this drawn line then, using the width of the walking foot as a guide, stitch vertical lines moving from the middle out towards the edge.

If you wish to quilt in straight lines on the diagonal, use a fabric marking pencil to draw a line from corner to corner. Stitch on the drawn line, then mark the next diagonal line in parallel to the first and stitch. Repeat across the project.

BINDING

You can either use a ready-made binding, or make your own from a matching or contrasting fabric.

Preparing the item for binding

Trim the excess backing and wadding (batting) level with the edge of the project. Make sure edges are straight and corners square or, if the shape is curved, that the seam allowance is even. If not, correct using a ruler and rotary cutter on a mat or sharp scissors.

Cutting the binding

If you want to make your own binding, cut strips from the chosen fabric, stitching them together, if necessary, to create one continuous strip of the length required.

If the item is straight-sided, you can use straight strips and join them on the straight or at a 45-degree angle.

If a project has curved edges it needs to be bound with bias binding. To cut bias strips, fold the fabric on the diagonal to make a triangle. Cut the strips to the required width across the diagonal, starting at the folded edge. The larger the folded triangle, the longer the bias strips. Stitch the strips together at a 45-degree angle to make the length required. Press the seams open to reduce bulk.

Sewing the binding

Fold your binding strip in half lengthways, wrong sides together, and press. Match the raw edges of the binding to the raw edge of the project and sew in place, smoothing around curves or folding the binding at 45 degrees at the corners so it lies flat. Fold the binding to the back of the item, turn under and slip stitch in place by hand.

CLIPPING CURVES

If your shapes are not straight-sided, clip the seam allowances from the edge close to the seam line using small, sharp scissors. This allows the fabric to lie flat when you press the seams.

FINISHING STITCHES

Slip stitching

A slip stitch is used to secure a finished edge, such as a hand appliquéd shape or binding, invisibly to another fabric. Catch a thread from under the fabric with a needle and a single thread on the fold of the fabric. Repeat along the seam, keeping the stitches as even as possible.

Top stitching

Many of the projects use top stitching as a decorative feature or to hold fast a finished edge, such as the top of a bag or a pocket. Neat and even top stitching improves the appearance of a project and often helps it to lay flat. Each pattern explains where to stitch, usuallly ⅛in (0.32cm) or ¼in (0.65cm) from the finished edge. You can use your standard presser foot on your sewing machine or a zipper or edge stitch foot. The key is keeping the distance from the finished edge even.

Stitching in the ditch

With this method you quilt in the seam lines. As the quilting sinks into the seam the result is a raised effect without distracting from the patterns created by the patchwork. The trick is to keep the quilting in the seam line and not wobble over the edge.

PROJECTS USING HEXAGONS

COASTERS

DESIGNED BY JANET GODDARD

These bright and cheerful coasters are not only useful but eye-catching as well. Hexagons are stitched together in a rosette design and then stitched to thick felt, which provides the heat protection for surfaces from the hot drinks.

SKILL LEVEL: BEGINNER

YOU'LL NEED

For each coaster

Templates
- Seven 1in (2.5cm) paper hexagons (page 138)

Fabric
Requirements based on fabrics with a useable width of 42in (107cm)
- 2½in (6.3cm) purple floral for the outer hexagons
- One 2½in (6.3cm) square plain purple for the middle hexagon
- One 7in (17.8cm) square of pink felt for the base

Haberdashery
- Purple and black thread for piecing
- Scissors, needle, pins
- Rotary cutter, ruler and mat (optional)

CUTTING

Purple floral fabric
- Six hexagons

Plain purple fabric
- One hexagon

FINISHED SIZE

6 × 6in (15.2 × 15.2cm)

METHOD

To stitch the EPP
1 Cut out and tack (baste) the hexagons and lay the floral hexagons out around the plain purple hexagon.

2 Whip stitch (page 20) one side of each floral hexagon to the middle hexagon.

3 Whip stitch the adjoining seams of each hexagon together. Press and remove the papers.

To finish the coaster
4 Lay the completed coaster on top of the 7in (17.8cm) square of pink felt, ensuring that it is placed in the middle. Pin in place.

5 Slip stitch (page 24) the outer edge of the hexagons to the felt square.

6 Carefully cut the felt away from the hexagons so that it makes a ¼in (0.65cm) frame around the fabric hexagons. Press.

5

> *Tip*
> To add additional insulation to the coasters, a double layer of felt could be used instead of one.

6

ZIPPY POUCH

DESIGNED BY JANET GODDARD

Stitch yourself a fun but functional zippy pouch suitable for storing those essential beauty items. EPP hexagons are stitched to a soft grey linen fabric, the pouch is lightly padded with fusible wadding, lined with an eye-catching print and finished with a zip.

SKILL LEVEL: CONFIDENT

YOU'LL NEED

Templates

- Nineteen 1in (2.5cm) paper hexagons (page 138)

Fabric

Requirements based on fabrics with a useable width of 42in (107cm)

- 11in (27.9cm) plain grey for the outer pouch
- 11in (27.9cm) heart print for the lining
- Fabric scraps in red, grey, pink, teal and white for the hexagons

Haberdashery

- 11in (27.9cm) fusible wadding (batting)
- One 10in (25cm) grey zip
- 4in (10cm) grey ribbon, ⅛in (0.32cm) wide for the zip pull
- Grey thread
- Scissors, needle, pins
- Rotary cutter, ruler and mat (optional)
- Sewing machine

CUTTING

Grey fabric

- Two 10½ × 9½in (26.7 × 24cm) rectangles

Heart print fabric

- Two 10½ × 9¼in (26.7 × 23.5cm) rectangles

Fabric scraps

- Four red hexagons
- Four grey hexagons
- Three teal hexagons
- Four pink hexagons
- Four white hexagons

Fusible wadding (batting)

- Two 10½ × 9½in (26.7 × 24cm) rectangles

FINISHED SIZE

10 × 9in (25 × 23cm)

METHOD

To stitch the EPP

1 Cut out and tack (baste) the nineteen hexagons and lay them out in three rows with six hexagons in the first row, seven in the second and six in the third, ensuring that the fabrics are alternated evenly across the three rows. Whip stitch (page 20) the hexagons in each row together, then stitch the three rows to each other.

2 Press and remove the papers.

To finish the zippy pouch

3 Take one 10½ × 9½in (26.7 × 24cm) grey rectangle and pin the EPP to the grey fabric, positioning the top row of the EPP 2in (5cm) from the raw edge of the fabric.

4 Slip stitch (page 24) the top and bottom rows of EPP to the grey fabric.

5 Trim the overhanging hexagons in line with the sides of the grey rectangle.

1

2

3
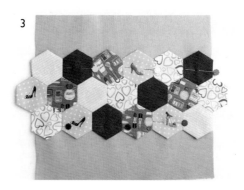

4
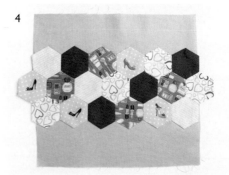

5
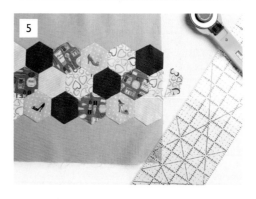

6 Iron the fusible wadding (batting) to the wrong side of each grey rectangle. On the rectangle that has the hexagons stitched to it, quilt (page 23) ¼in (0.65cm) away from the top and bottom hexagons, following the line of hexagons.

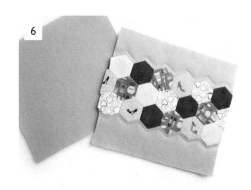

7 To attach the zip, place the first outer pouch section right side up and place the zip face down on the front, matching the top edge. Pin in place and then pin the 10½ × 9¼in (26.7 × 23.5cm) heart print rectangle on top, right side down. Machine stitch along the top edge to secure the lining, zip and outer pouch.

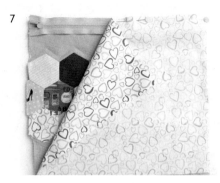

8 Repeat to attach the zip to the second pouch section. Open out each panel and press. Machine stitch ⅛in (0.32cm) each side of the zip with the grey thread.

9 Open the zip halfway and place the two outer pouch sections right sides together and also the lining panels right sides together. Pin and machine stitch all the way around the edge, leaving a 3in (7.6cm) gap in the stitching in the bottom of the lining.

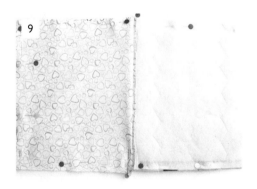

10 Clip the corners and turn the pouch through the opening in the lining so it is right side out. Slip stitch the opening closed. Press well. To finish, tie the ribbon to the zip pull.

Tip
The EPP hexagons feature make-up and shoe-related images but they could be substituted with alternative motifs if the pouch was to be used for a different purpose.

LAVENDER BAG

DESIGNED BY JANET GODDARD

A delicate little bag perfect for filling with dried lavender. A great project for using up those precious tiny fabric scraps, I have used pieces of Liberty fabric here. The bag features a circle of little hexagons and is decorated with lace trim and finished with a ribbon.

SKILL LEVEL: BEGINNER

YOU'LL NEED

Templates
- Six ½in (1.3cm) paper hexagons (page 138)

Fabric
Requirements based on fabrics with a useable width of 42in (107cm)
- 9in (23cm) cream for the bag
- Fabric scraps in red and cream floral for the hexagons

Haberdashery
- 9in (23cm) cream lace, 1in (2.5cm) wide for the top of the bag
- 15in (38.1cm) red ribbon, ⅛in (0.32cm) wide for the tie
- Cream thread
- Scissors, needle, pins
- Rotary cutter, ruler and mat (optional)
- Sewing machine
- Lavender to fill

CUTTING

Cream fabric
- One 9 × 9in (23 × 23cm) square

Fabric scraps
- Three red floral hexagons
- Three cream floral hexagons

FINISHED SIZE

4¼ × 8½in (10.8 × 21.6cm)

METHOD

To stitch the EPP

1 Cut out and tack (baste) the six hexagons and lay them out in a ring, alternating the red and cream floral fabrics.

2 Whip stitch (page 20) the hexagons together by stitching one side of each hexagon to the next hexagon. Press and remove the papers.

To finish the lavender bag

3 Take the 9 × 9in (23 × 23cm) cream square and position the EPP 1½in (3.8cm) up from the bottom in the middle of the square. Slip stitch (page 24) the EPP in place.

4 Press under a ¼in (0.65cm) seam to the reverse of the fabric at the top of the cream square. Working on the reverse of the fabric, machine stitch one edge of the lace over the pressed ¼in (0.65cm) edge. To attach the ribbon tie, take the ribbon and fold it in half. Place the centre fold of the ribbon on one side of the right side of the cream square 2in (5cm) from the top edge of the fabric. Stitch this in place with an ⅛in (0.32cm) seam.

5 With right sides together, place the long sides on top of each other and machine stitch together, being careful not to catch the ends of the ribbon in the seam.

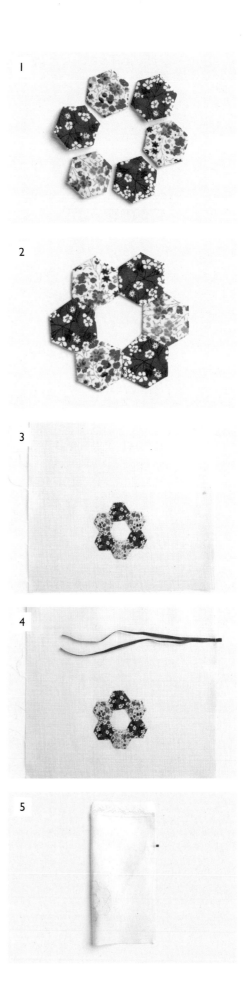

6 Move the side seam to the middle of the bag, ensuring that it is positioned exactly in the middle, and machine stitch across the bottom of the bag. Trim the corners.

7 Turn the bag through to the right side and press well. Fill with lavender and tie securely with the ribbon.

6

7

Tip
This is such a useful little bag which could be used as a gift bag if you didn't wish to use it for lavender.

BROOCH

DESIGNED BY JANET GODDARD

A tiny circle of hexagons in bright sunny fabrics stitched into a little brooch, this is perfect to add a splash of colour to a coat or jacket.

SKILL LEVEL: BEGINNER

YOU'LL NEED

Templates
- Seven ½in (1.3cm) paper hexagons (page 138)

Fabric
- Fabric scraps in yellow and black for the hexagons
- One 3½in (8.9cm) square of black felt for the brooch back

Haberdashery
- Yellow and black thread
- One metal brooch pin, 1in (2.5cm) in length
- Scissors, needle, pins
- Rotary cutter, ruler and mat (optional)

CUTTING

Yellow fabric
- Six hexagons

Black fabric
- One hexagon

FINISHED SIZE

2¾ × 2¾in (7 × 7cm)

METHOD

To stitch the EPP

1 Cut out and tack (baste) the hexagons and lay out the six yellow hexagons in a ring around the black hexagon.

2 Whip stitch (page 20) the hexagons together by stitching one side of each hexagon to the middle hexagon. Stitch the adjoining seams of each hexagon together. Press and remove the papers.

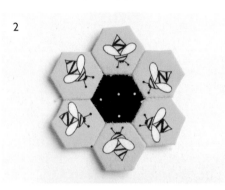

To finish the brooch

3 Lay the completed brooch on top of the 3½in (8.9cm) square of black felt, ensuring that it is placed in the middle. Pin in place. Slip stitch (page 24) the outer edge of the hexagons to the felt square.

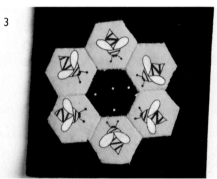

4 Carefully cut the felt away from the hexagons so that it is ¼in (0.65cm) away from the outer edge of the fabric hexagons. Press.

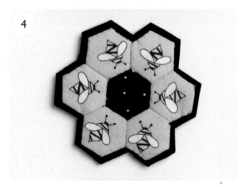

5 Stitch the brooch pin to the reverse of the brooch, ensuring that the stitches only go through the felt and not the hexagons.

> *Tip*
> I have fussy cut (page 17) the fabrics for the yellow hexagons to showcase a little bee on each segment, which gives the brooch a nice focal point.

PROJECTS USING DIAMONDS

TEA COSY
DESIGNED BY JEMIMA SCHLEE

Keep your brew lovely and warm with this pretty tea cosy. You can choose whether to decorate one side, as I have done, or double the number of diamonds and decorate both sides. Create the perfect size to fit your tea pot by altering the size of the base fabric – make your own template using newspaper or scrap paper and a stapler to ensure your tea pot will be nice and snug.

SKILL LEVEL: CONFIDENT

YOU'LL NEED

Templates
- Eleven 3in (7.6cm) paper six-point diamonds (page 138)
- One 3in (7.6cm) half-length paper six-point diamonds (page 138)
- Two 3in (7.6cm) quarter paper six-point diamonds (page 138)

Fabric
Requirements based on fabrics with a useable width of 42in (107cm)
- 15in (38.1cm) plain fabric for the base
- 15in (38.1cm) plain calico for the lining
- 10in (25cm) plain teal fabric for the diamonds
- Fabric scraps in pink pattern for the diamonds

Haberdashery
- 15in (38.1cm) wadding (batting)
- White thread for piecing
- Thread to match your fabrics
- Quilting needle and quilting thread
- Scissors, needle, pins
- Rotary cutter, ruler and mat (optional)
- Sewing machine

CUTTING

Plain base fabric

- Two pieces cut from the template (see page 138)

Lining fabric

- Two pieces cut from the template (see page 138)

Plain teal fabric

- Five 3½in (8.9cm) six-point diamonds
- One 3½in (8.9cm) half-length six-point diamond
- Two 3½in (8.9cm) quarter six-point diamonds

Patterned fabric scraps

- Six 3½in (8.9cm) six-point diamonds

Wadding (batting)

- Two pieces cut from the template (see page 138)

FINISHED SIZE

11½ × 12in (29 × 30.5cm)

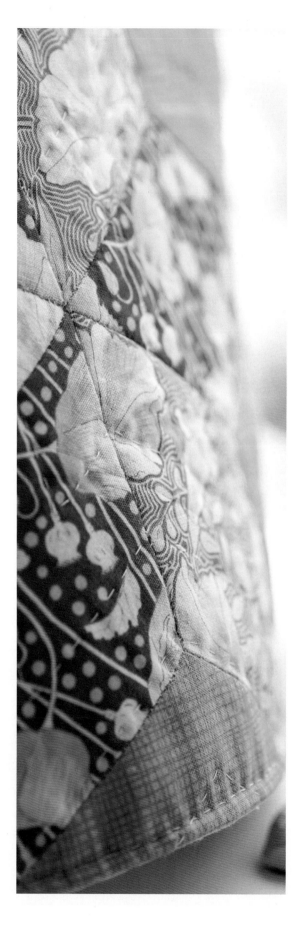

METHOD

To stitch the EPP

1 Cut out and tack (baste) all your EPP pieces and lay them down following the design layout.

2 Piece your EPPs together, filling the edge gaps with the half-length and quarter diamond pieces. Press with a hot iron.

To finish the tea cosy

3 Carefully take your papers out by snipping the thread. Fold the raw seam allowance all the way round back in and press. Lay one piece of wadding on one piece of your base fabric, leaving an even gap between the two all the way around. Pin or tack in place and top stitch (page 24) ⅛in (0.32cm) inside the edge of the wadding. Do the same with the second piece. Remove any pins or tacking (basting). Take one base piece and place it right side up in front of you. Place your EPP on top of your base fabric, sitting just ⅛in (0.32cm) from the bottom edge and centred between the left- and right-hand edges. Tack the two layers of fabric together around the circumference.

4 Use a needle and white thread to appliqué your EPP to the base around its outside edge – it is not necessary to stitch along the bottom. Now quilt your EPP with star shapes following the template on page 141.

5 Place your two pieces of base fabric right sides together and pin or tack aligning the raw side edges but leaving the bottom open. Stitch a ⅜in (1cm) seam around the four side edges of your work.

1

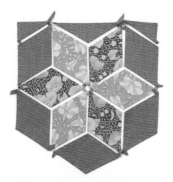

2

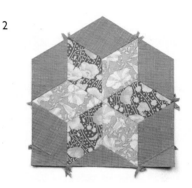

3

4

5

6 Do the same with the two pieces of lining fabric. Turn your quilted outer right sides out and push down into the lining that is still inside out so that the sections are right sides together.

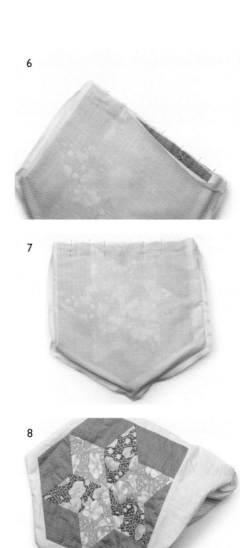

7 Align the raw edges and pin or tack them together.

8 Stitch a ¼in (0.65cm) seam by machine around this edge, remembering to leave a turning gap. Turn your work right sides out through the turning gap and push the lining up inside the tea cosy.

9 Fold in the seam allowance at the turning gap and close it with small whip stitches (page 20). Make a line of quilting (page 23) through all layers of fabric around ⅛in (0.32cm) in from the bottom edge.

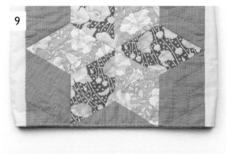

> *Tip*
> A six-point diamond has an angle of 60 degrees and its size is the length of one side. A five-point diamond has an angle of 72 degrees and an eight-point has an angle of 45 degrees.

TABLE MAT

DESIGNED BY JEMIMA SCHLEE

This bold, graphic pattern can look very contemporary by using fabrics with strong colours and patterns. Make one to use as a trivet for hot pots and serving dishes, or make a set for place mats. It's a great project for using up scraps from your stash, and by using a mix of patterned fabrics you can create a more eclectic feel, making the design softer.

SKILL LEVEL: BEGINNER

YOU'LL NEED

Templates
- Seventeen 3in (7.6cm) paper six-point diamonds (page 138)
- Three 3in (7.6cm) half-length paper six-point diamonds (page 138)
- Two 3in (7.6cm) half-width paper six-point diamonds (page 139)
- Six 3in (7.6cm) quarter paper six-point diamonds (page 138)

Fabric
Requirements based on fabrics with a useable width of 42in (107cm)
- 12in (30.5cm) fabric of choice for the backing
- Fabric scraps in lime yellow (light), green (medium) and purple patterned (dark) for the diamonds (see tip on page 50)

Haberdashery
- 12in (30.5cm) quilt wadding (batting) (or thermal wadding – see tip on page 50)
- Bias binding 60in (150cm), ½in (1.3cm) wide
- White thread for piecing (or black if your piecing fabrics are quite dark)
- Thread to match your patched fabrics (or a colour of your choice depending on how visible you want your quilting to be)
- Quilting needle and quilting thread
- Fabric shears
- Scissors, needle, pins
- Rotary cutter, ruler and mat (optional)
- Sewing machine

CUTTING

All cutting instructions include a ¼in (0.65cm) seam allowance unless otherwise stated.

Backing fabric

- One 16¼ × 10½in (41.3 × 26.7cm) rectangle

Plain lime yellow fabric scraps (light)

- Five 3½in (8.9cm) six-point diamonds
- Three 3½in (8.9cm) half-length six-point diamonds
- Two 3½in (8.9cm) half-width six-point diamonds

Plain grey fabric scraps (medium)

- Six 3½in (8.9cm) six-point diamonds
- Three 3½in (8.9cm) quarter six-point diamonds

Patterned fabric scraps (dark)

- Six 3½in (8.9cm) six-point diamonds
- Three 3½in (8.9cm) quarter six-point diamonds

Wadding (or thermal wadding)

- One 16¼ × 10½in (41.3 × 26.7cm) rectangle

FINISHED SIZE

15¾ × 10¾in (40 × 26.9cm)

METHOD

To stitch the EPP

1 Cut out and tack (baste) all your EPP diamonds and lay them down following the design layout.

2 Take one each of a dark and medium diamond and whip stitch (page 20) together to form a chevron shape. Take a light diamond and stitch it to the dark and medium connected diamonds to form an isometric cube. Continue in this fashion until all your pieces are stitched together. Fill the edge gaps with the half-length, half-width and quarter diamond pieces. Give your work a press with a hot iron.

3 Carefully take your papers out by snipping the thread. The joining seams should remain pressed open, the raw edges must be unfolded and pressed flat. Give your work another good press with a hot iron. Try hard not to stretch the edges of the fabric – if your sewing machine is right there, you can top stitch (page 24) very close to the edge to ensure this.

To finish the table mat

4 Lay your backing fabric right side down. Place your wadding on top, aligning the raw edges, and pin together.

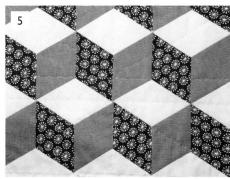

5 Lay your pieced top right side up centrally on the wadding attached to the backing. You will have extra wadding and backing extending around all the edges of your pieced work. Press again before pinning around the edges. Tack (baste) the three layers of fabric together, tacking from the centre of your work out to the edges in a sunray pattern, smoothing out the fabric as you go to minimize wrinkles. Now use a needle and thread to quilt your work (page 23).

6 Trim all the excess wadding and backing with sharp sewing shears, cutting them flush with the raw edge of the EPP.

7 Finally, finish off your mat with bias binding by machine or hand (page 23).

Tips
When choosing fabrics, this project works best with dark, medium and light tones. Screw your eyes up slightly to help you define the difference in tones if using several patterned fabrics, or simply use plains.

Substituting the wadding for thermal wadding adds extra protection for your surfaces.

OVEN PAD

DESIGNED BY JEMIMA SCHLEE

This lovely oven pad is lined with thermal wadding for extra protection. Made with hot colours and quilted with squares, it makes a great housewarming gift. Choose darker colours to minimize the stubborn stains that come from kitchen use. Think about using a contrast colour for your quilting stitch to add extra interest.

SKILL LEVEL: BEGINNER

YOU'LL NEED

Templates
- Eight 3in (7.6cm) paper eight-point diamonds (page 138)
- Eight 2¼in (5.7cm) half-square paper triangles (page 138)

Fabric
Requirements based on fabrics with a useable width of 42in (107cm)
- 10in (25cm) purple floral for the backing
- Fabric scraps in three shades of orange colours and patterns for the diamonds and half-square triangles

Haberdashery
- 10in (25cm) thermal wadding (batting)
- Bias binding 40in (1m), ½in (1.3cm) wide
- Black thread for piecing (or white if your piecing fabrics are quite light)
- Quilting needle and quilting thread
- Scissors, needle, pins
- Rotary cutter, ruler and mat (optional)
- Sewing machine

CUTTING

Purple floral fabric
- One 9 × 9in (23 × 23cm) square

Orange fabric scraps
- Eight 3½in (8.9cm) eight-point diamonds
- Eight 2¾in (5.7cm) half-square triangles

Wadding
- One 9 × 9in (23 × 23cm) square

FINISHED SIZE

8¾ × 8¾in (22.2 × 22.2cm)

METHOD

To stitch the EPP

1 Cut out and tack (baste) all your EPP pieces and lay them down following the design layout.

2 Piece your EPPs together using a whip stitch (page 20), filling the edge gaps with the half-length, half-width and quarter diamond pieces.

To finish the oven pad

3 Remove your EPP papers carefully. Give your work a press with a hot iron, turning all the edge seam allowances out and pressing them open. Press your backing fabric. Lay it down wrong side up (if it has a right and wrong side). Lay your square of wadding or thermal wadding on top of it, aligning the raw edges all the way round.

4 Place your pieced work on top and in the middle so that any excess of backing and wadding (batting) is extending the same amount on all sides.

Tip
An eight-point diamond has an angle of 45 degrees and eight will fit together to make a star with their points at the centre of a circle.

5 Tack the three layers of fabric together, tacking from the middle of your work out to the edges in a sunray pattern, smoothing out the fabric as you go to minimize wrinkles. Now use a quilting needle and quilting thread to quilt (page 23) your work. I used a simple grid.

6 Trim all the excess wadding and backing, cutting them flush with the raw edge of the EPP. Finally, finish off your mat with bias binding by machine or hand (page 23).

5

6
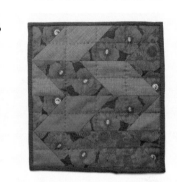

COFFEE COSY

DESIGNED BY JANET GODDARD

There is nothing better than a steaming hot cup of coffee and this cheerful cosy wraps around the cafetière to keep your coffee piping hot so giving you plenty of time for a second cup. This project is decorated with a star design and insulated with wadding (batting).

SKILL LEVEL: BEGINNER

YOU'LL NEED

Templates
- Twelve 1in (2.5cm) paper six-point diamonds (page 138)

Fabric
Requirements based on fabrics with a useable width of 42in (107cm)
- 5in (12.7cm) turquoise stripe for the cosy outer and lining
- Fabric scraps in blue and green for the diamonds

Haberdashery
- 5in (12.7cm) insulated fusible wadding (batting)
- 3½in (8.9cm) strip of sew-on hook and loop tape, 1in (2.5cm) wide
- Turquoise thread for piecing
- Scissors, needle, pins
- Rotary cutter, ruler and mat (optional)
- Sewing machine (optional)

CUTTING

Turquoise stripe fabric
- Two 14 × 4¾in (35.6 × 12cm) rectangles

Fabric scraps
- Six blue diamonds
- Six green diamonds

Fusible wadding (batting)
- One 14 × 4¾in (35.6 × 12cm) rectangle

FINISHED SIZE

13½ × 4¼in (34.3 × 10.8cm)

METHOD

To stitch the EPP

1 Cut out and tack (baste) the twelve diamonds and lay them out into two star designs, alternating the green and blue colours.

2 To make one star, whip stitch (page 20) six diamonds together by stitching one side of each diamond to another until all six are stitched together. Repeat for the second star.

To finish the coffee cosy

3 Press the stars and remove the papers. Take one of the 14 × 4¾in (35.6 × 12cm) turquoise rectangles and position the EPP stars in the middle on the right side of the rectangle 1in (2.5cm) away from the outer long edges and 2½in (6.3cm) away from the short edges. Slip stitch (page 24) in place.

4 Take half of the hook and loop tape and stitch it to the left side of the second 14 × 4¾in (35.6 × 12cm) turquoise rectangle, ½in (1.3cm) in from the edge of one short end.

5 Iron the fusible wadding (batting) to the wrong side of the turquoise rectangle completed in step 4.

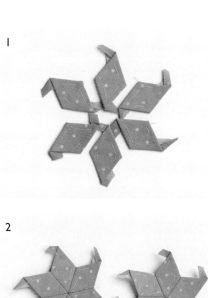

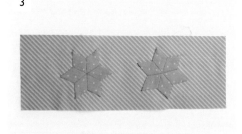

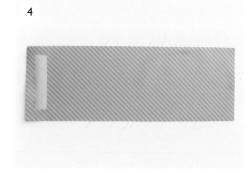

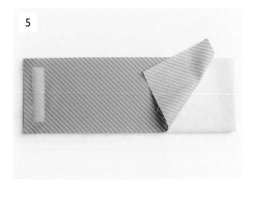

6 With right sides together, place the unit completed in step 3 on top of the unit completed in step 5, pin and stitch around each side, leaving a 2½in (6.3cm) gap in the stitching on one long edge. Trim the corners.

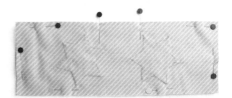

7 Turn the cosy through the gap so it is right side out. Press carefully, avoiding the hook and loop and top stitch (page 24) around each side ⅛in (0.32cm) in from the edge, closing the opening as you go.

8 Stitch the second half of the hook and loop tape to the short edge of the outer cosy, on the opposite end to the other strip of tape, making sure it is on the opposite side.

Tip
The measurements for this coffee cosy fit a six-cup cafetière with the edges overlapping by 1½in (3.8cm) which gives the cover a snug fit. Before starting the project, measure your cafetière to ensure that the cosy will fit. If it doesn't, adjust the measurements accordingly.

STORAGE BASKET

DESIGNED BY JANET GODDARD

An attractive little basket which will look perfect on a shelf as well as providing handy storage for sewing supplies, stationery or cosmetics. The basket has a contrasting fabric lining, wadding (batting) and useful fabric handles.

SKILL LEVEL: CONFIDENT

YOU'LL NEED

Templates
- Six 1in (2.5cm) paper six-point diamonds (page 138)

Fabric
Requirements based on fabrics with a useable width of 42in (107cm)
- 10in (25cm) cream for the outer basket
- 10in (25cm) rust for the inner basket, handles and diamonds

Haberdashery
- 10in (25cm) fusible wadding (batting)
- Cream and rust thread
- Scissors, needle, pins
- Rotary cutter, ruler and mat (optional)
- Sewing machine (optional)

CUTTING

Cream fabric
- One 9½ × 12in (24 × 30.5cm) rectangle

Rust fabric
- One 9½ × 11½in (24 × 29cm) rectangle
- One 3½ × 11½in (8.9 × 29cm) strip
- Six diamonds

Fusible wadding (batting)
- One 9½ × 12in (24 × 30.5cm) rectangle

FINISHED SIZE

9 × 4½ × 2¼in (23 × 11.4 × 5.7cm)

METHOD

To stitch the EPP
1 Cut out and tack (baste) the six diamonds and lay them out in a star design.

2 Whip stitch (page 20) the diamonds together by stitching one side of each diamond to another until all six are stitched together. Press and remove the papers.

To finish the storage basket
3 Take the 9½ × 12in (24 × 30.5cm) cream rectangle and position the EPP star centrally on the right side of the rectangle 1in (2.5cm) away from one 9½in (24cm) edge. Slip stitch (page 24) in place.

4 Iron the fusible wadding (batting) to the wrong side of the unit completed in step 3.

1

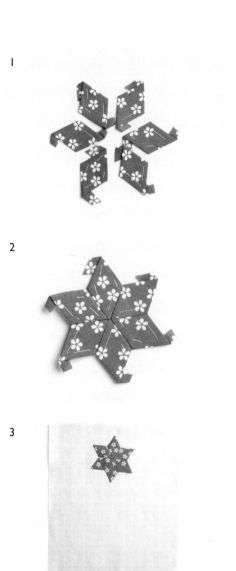

2

3

4

5 Fold the basket in half with right sides together bringing the 9½in (24cm) sides together, and stitch down each side. To shape the base, match the fold with the side seam. Measure in 1¼in (3.2cm) along the seam line and stitch across.

6 Cut off the excess fabric at the corner. Repeat to sew across the opposite corner and cut off the excess fabric, then turn through.

7 To make the handles, take the 3½ × 11½in (8.9 × 29cm) rust strip and press under ¼in (0.65cm) along each long side. Fold the strip of fabric wrong sides together so that the folded edges meet. Stitch ⅛in (0.32cm) away from the folded edge. Stitch ⅛in (0.32cm) away from the long edge on the other side.

8 Cut the strip stitched in step 7 in half to make two handles. Take the basket and, with right sides facing, place the raw edges of each handle on either side of the basket side seam. Pin and then stitch the handles to the basket using an ⅛in (0.32cm) seam.

5

6

7

8

9 To stitch the lining, take the 9½ × 11½in (24 × 29cm) rust rectangle and fold in half, right sides facing, with the 9½in (24cm) opening at the top. Stitch down each side but leave a 2½in (6.3cm) gap in stitching on one side approximately 1½in (3.8cm) from the top.

10 To shape the lining corners, repeat the instructions in steps 5 and 6. Turn the outer basket so that the wadding (batting) is facing outwards. Put the lining inside the basket so that the right side of the lining is facing the right side of the basket.

11 Pin around the top, matching the side seams, and then stitch all the way around. Turn the basket through the gap in the stitching in the lining. Push out the corners and slip stitch (page 24) the gap closed. Pull the lining up so that it sits ¼in (0.65cm) above the cream fabric. Press and stitch in the seam line between the rust and cream fabrics (page 24).

PROJECTS USING TRIANGLES

PENCIL CASE

DESIGNED BY JEMIMA SCHLEE

A zipped bag to organize your pens, scissors and stationery bits and bobs, this project produces a very useful make. You can adjust the size fairly simply, and the choice of fabric colour, pattern and tone can produce a case with a unique character. Is it just a pencil case? Not at all! This little bag can equally double up as a make-up bag, somewhere to keep a first aid kit, or many other uses.

SKILL LEVEL: CONFIDENT

YOU'LL NEED

Templates
- Fourteen 3in (7.6cm) paper equilateral triangles (page 139)

Fabric
Requirements based on fabrics with a useable width of 42in (107cm)
- 12in (30.5cm) purple pattern for the body
- Fabric scraps in four different colours for equilateral triangles

Haberdashery
- 8in (20.3cm) zip
- White thread
- Thread to match your fabric
- Fabric shears
- Scissors, needle, pins
- Rotary cutter, ruler and mat (optional)
- Sewing machine
- Zipper foot

CUTTING

Purple pattern fabric
- Two 11 × 7in (27.9 × 17.8cm) rectangles base fabric for outer, this includes ⅜in (1cm) seam allowance

Fabric scraps
- Fourteen 3½in (8.9cm) equilateral triangles in four colours

FINISHED SIZE

10½ × 6in (26.7 × 15.2cm)

METHOD

To stitch the EPP

1 Cut out and tack (baste) all your triangles. Lay them out in order before piecing them together.

2 Once the triangles are pieced together into two strips, sew the strips together into a long line of triangles, then join them into a loop.

3 Now stitch two edges of the 'belt' together along the bottom edge to create a 'boat' of EPPs. Press with a hot iron.

4 Carefully take your papers out of your EPP by snipping the thread. Give your work a good press with a hot iron. Fold the seam allowance in along the top raw edge and tack in place.

To finish the pencil case

5 Lay your base fabric down right side up in front of you. Lay your zip right side down, centred along one short edge, aligning the top edge of the zip to the raw edge of the fabric. Pin along the bottom edge of the zip before stitching along just above the teeth, ¼in (0.65cm) from the edge.

1
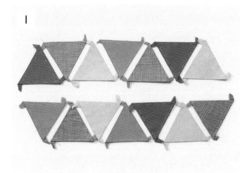

2

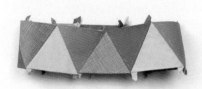

3

4
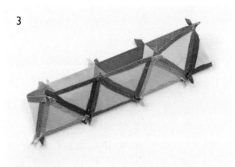

5

6 Remove the pins or tacking, fold the fabric back away from the zip and press.

7 Place the second base fabric piece face up in front of you and put the other piece with the zip attached face down on top of it, zip at the top. Align the top edge of the zip to the top raw edge of the base fabric. Pin or tack in place before machine stitching as before.

8 Press your work and top stitch (page 24) around your zip on the right side of your work.

6

7

8

9 Place your work right sides together, aligning the raw edges and making sure your zip is open before you start stitching. Stitch ⅜in (1cm) seam around the three sides, You can zigzag along the edges to reduce fraying.

10 Turn your work right sides out and press with a hot iron. Take your prepared pencil case body and push its base down inside the EPP, making sure the two bottom corners are pushed snuggly in. Pin or tack around the top edge of the EPP to attach it to the base fabric – take care not to stitch through both layers of the base fabric by placing one hand inside the pencil case whilst you do this.

11 Quilt (page 23) just inside the seams of all the equilateral triangles, continuing to keep one hand inside the pencil case to avoid stitching through too many layers of fabric.

TABLET STORAGE

DESIGNED BY JANET GODDARD

Keep your tablet safe when out and about with this softly padded case. The bright and cheerful fabrics in a triangle design will ensure that you never misplace your tablet again. The case is quilted, which not only gives it texture but the additional padding provides great protection for your device. Before you start, check the dimensions are correct for your tablet (see tip on page 74).

SKILL LEVEL: BEGINNER

YOU'LL NEED

Templates
- Twenty-four 2½in (6.3cm) paper half-square triangles (page 138)

Fabric
Requirements based on fabrics with a useable width of 42in (107cm)
- 9in (23cm) turquoise for the outer back
- 9in (23cm) turquoise spot for the lining
- Fabric scraps in bright colours for the front

Haberdashery
- 9in (23cm) fusible wadding (batting)
- 18in (45.7cm) turquoise ribbon, ¼in (0.65cm) wide
- One button, ½in (1.3cm) diameter
- Grey thread for piecing and quilting
- Scissors, needle, pins
- Rotary cutter, ruler and mat (optional)
- Sewing machine (optional)

CUTTING

Turquoise fabric
- One 8 × 10½in (20.3 × 26.7cm) rectangle

Turquoise spot fabric
- Two 8 × 10½in (20.3 × 26.7cm) rectangles

Fabric scraps
- Twelve 3½in (8.9cm) squares, crosscut each of these on the diagonal once to yield twenty-four triangles

Fusible wadding (batting)
- One 8 × 10½in (20.3 × 26.7cm) rectangle

FINISHED SIZE

7½ × 10in (19 × 25cm)

METHOD

To stitch the EPP

1 Cut out and tack (baste) the triangles. Whip stitch (page 20) the triangles together in pairs, joining the diagonals together.

2 Whip stitch the units from step 1 together into four rows of six triangles, ensuring that the diagonal seams all go in the same direction.

3 Whip stitch the rows together.

To finish the tablet case

4 Press and remove the papers. Press the outer edge seam allowance flat and away from the triangles. Iron the fusible wadding (batting) to the wrong side of this unit. Iron the fusible wadding to the wrong side of the 8 × 10½in (20.3 × 26.7cm) turquoise rectangle.

5 Quilt (page 23) diagonal lines across the patchwork outer front ½in (1.3cm) away from the seam lines through both the fabric and the wadding (batting).

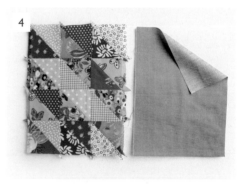

6 Quilt diagonal lines 2in (5cm) apart across the turquoise outer back through both the fabric and the wadding.

7 Take the strip of ribbon and fold it in half. Stitch the fold to the centre of one 8in (20.3cm) end of the unit completed in step 6 with an ⅛in (0.32cm) seam.

8 Place the two quilted units right sides together and stitch up each long side and across the short side that is opposite to the one where the ribbon is stitched. Trim the corners and turn through.

9 To stitch the lining, place the two 8 × 10½in (20.3 × 26.7cm) turquoise spot rectangles right sides together and stitch up each long side and across one short side, leaving a 3in (7.6cm) gap in stitching in the middle of one side. Trim the corners neatly.

6

7

8

9

10 Place the outer tablet case right side facing out, inside the lining, right sides together. Pin all the way around the top edge, matching the side seams. Stitch. Turn the case right side out through the opening in the lining. Stitch the opening closed with small neat slip stitches (page 24).

11 Carefully press the top of the tablet case so that ¼in (0.65cm) of the lining is showing on the outside, then pin in place. Stitch through all layers in the seam line around the top. Stitch the button to the front of the case 1in (2.5cm) from the top edge in the middle. Tie the ribbon around the button.

Tip
The size of the tablet case can be adjusted to fit a device of any size. Simply measure the width and length of your tablet and add 2in (5cm) to these measurements.

NOTEBOOK COVER

DESIGNED BY JANET GODDARD

Turn an ordinary notebook into a treasured possession with this embellished notebook cover. The beauty of having a personalized cover is that once your notebook is full of lists, notes or reminders, you can simply take off the cover and re-use it on your next notebook.

SKILL LEVEL: BEGINNER

YOU'LL NEED

Templates
- Twelve 1½in (3.8cm) paper equilateral triangles (page 139)

Fabric
Requirements based on fabrics with a useable width of 42in (107cm)
- 10in (25cm) heart print for the notebook outer and flaps
- 10in (25cm) pink for the lining
- Fabric scraps in grey and red for the triangles

Haberdashery
- 10in (25cm) fusible interfacing
- 6 × 8½in (15.2 × 21.6cm) notebook
- Grey thread for piecing
- Scissors, needle, pins
- Rotary cutter, ruler and mat (optional)
- Sewing machine

CUTTING

Heart print fabric
- One 13½ × 9½in (34.3 × 24cm) rectangle
- Two 7½ × 9½in (19 × 24cm) rectangles

Pink fabric
- One 13½ × 9½in (34.3 × 24cm) rectangle

Fabric scraps
- Six grey triangles
- Six red triangles

Fusible interfacing
- One 13½ × 9½in (34.3 × 24cm) rectangle

FINISHED SIZE

6¼ × 8¾in (15.9 × 22.2cm)

> *Tip*
> Before you start, measure your notebook and adjust the size of the cover if necessary.

METHOD

To stitch the EPP

1 Cut out and tack (baste) the twelve triangles and lay them out into one long strip, alternating the red and grey colours.

2 Whip stitch (page 20) the triangles together by stitching one side of each triangle to another until all twelve are stitched together in one flat strip. Press and remove the papers.

To finish the notebook cover

3 Take the heart print rectangle and position the strip of EPP triangles vertically 3½in (8.9cm) in from one short edge. Slip stitch (page 24) in place.

4 Trim away any overhanging part EPP triangles. Iron the fusible interfacing to the reverse of the unit completed in step 3.

5 To make the inner flaps, fold each of the 7½ × 9½in (19 × 24cm) heart print rectangles in half vertically, wrong sides together, and press. Place an inner flap on each end of the right side of the notebook cover; so that the raw edges line up and the folded edge faces the middle, and pin around the outer edges.

1

2

3

4

5
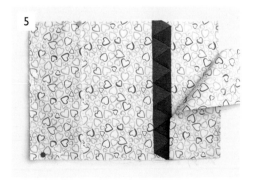

6 Lay the 13½ × 9½in (34.3 × 24cm) pink rectangle on top of the cover, right sides together. Pin around the outer edge, then stitch around all four sides, leaving a 3in (7.6cm) opening in the stitching on one long side. Trim the corners.

7 Turn the cover through the gap so that it is right side out. Push out the corners and give it a press. Slip stitch (page 24) the opening closed.

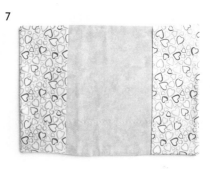

8 Add the notebook to the cover, slipping the front and back pages of the notebook under the fabric flaps.

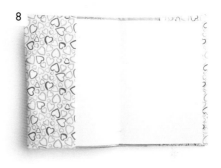

Tip
Fabric notebook covers make great personalized gifts and can be further embellished with embroidered names.

PHONE CASE

DESIGNED BY JEMIMA SCHLEE

A patched and padded case to protect your phone, just add a pair of half-square triangles at step 1 and change the fabric widths at step 3 to adapt the size to fit any phone. The measurements of each outer rectangle should be the circumference of your phone plus about ½in (1.3cm). Add more pairs of half-square triangles for taller phones. If in doubt, make your outer first and make it larger rather than too small.

SKILL LEVEL: BEGINNER

YOU'LL NEED

Templates
- Sixteen 1½in (3.8cm) paper half-square triangles (page 139)

Fabric
Requirements based on fabrics with a useable width of 42in (107cm)
- 10in (25cm) plain blue fabric for the front
- 10in (25cm) plain fabric for the lining
- Fabric scraps in plain fabric and contrasting patterned fabric for the half-square triangles

Haberdashery
- 6in (15.2cm) of wadding (batting)
- White thread
- Thread for matching fabrics
- Scissors, needle, pins
- Rotary cutter, ruler and mat (optional)
- Sewing machine

CUTTING

Blue fabric
- 10 × 20in (25 × 50.4cm) for the front

Plain lining
- 10 × 20in (25 × 50.4cm) rectangle

Fabric scraps
- Eight plain half-square triangles
- Eight patterned half-square triangles

Wadding (batting)
- 5 × 14in (12.7 × 35.6cm) rectangle

FINISHED SIZE

6 × 3¾in (15.2 × 9.5cm)

To fit phone size:
5 × 3½ (12.7 × 8.9cm)

METHOD

To stitch the EPP

1 Cut and tack (baste) your fabric to your EPP pieces and lay them out in position.

2 Working in one long strip, sew the pieces together with whip stitch (page 20). Give your work a good press with a hot iron.

To finish the phone case

3 Carefully remove the papers and press all the raw ¼in (0.65cm) edges open. Take one of your two narrow strips of main fabric and place it right sides down on top of your EPP, aligning their long raw edges. Pin or tack in place before machine stitching a ¼in (0.65cm) seam. Repeat with the second strip of main fabric. Remove the pins or tacking and press both seams towards the main fabric with a hot iron.

4 Lay your wadding (batting) to the back of your EPP piece, centred along its length, and tack into position.

5 Quilt (page 23) along either side of the pieced strip, stitching on the side of the main fabric.

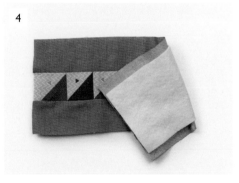

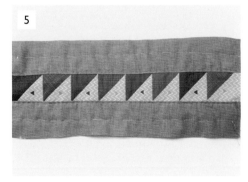

6 Lay your lining fabric down right side up. Place your EPP outer piece right side down on top of it, aligning the top short end of both. Pin or tack in position and stitch the short ends together by machine using a ¼in (0.65cm) seam. Do the same with the bottom short ends of these two pieces, creating a loop of fabric.

7 Press the seams from step 6 to the lining side of your work. Fold the loop of fabric in half, aligning the end of the seams from step 6. Pin or tack along each side before stitching ¼in (0.65cm) seams along both sides, remembering to leave a 2½in (6.3cm) turning gap along one edge of the lining. Reverse stitch at either side of the gap to strengthen it.

8 Carefully turn your work out through the turning gap.

9 Turn in the ¼in (0.65cm) seam allowance at the turning gap and close it with small, neat slip stitches (page 24).

10 Pick at the top corners of the outside of your case carefully with a pin to make them as sharp as possible. Push the lining down inside the outer. Give your work a good press and quilt (page 23) around the top edge of the case.

6
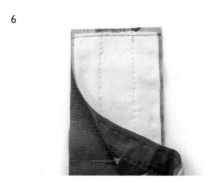

7

8

9

10

DOOR STOP

DESIGNED BY JEMIMA SCHLEE

Combine patterned and plain triangles in this satisfying 3-D project to create a pyramid to hold a door open. Personalize your design with bold prints or subtle shades. To check the minimum weight to make it effective, fill a plastic bag with grains until it is heavy enough to keep the door open. Scale it up by adding an extra row of triangles to the long bottom edge and enlarging your triangle base.

SKILL LEVEL: BEGINNER

YOU'LL NEED

Templates
- Twelve 3in (7.6cm) paper equilateral triangles (page 139)
- One 6in (15.2cm) paper equilateral triangle (page 139)

Fabric
Requirements based on fabrics with a useable width of 42in (107cm)
- 8in (20.3cm) plain fabric for the base
- 10in (25cm) fine calico for the lining
- Fabric scraps in bright colours and patterns for the triangles

Haberdashery
- White thread
- Thread to match your fabrics
- Scissors, needle, pins
- Rotary cutter, ruler and mat (optional)
- Sewing machine
- About 14oz (400g) dried lentils, beans or raw rice

CUTTING

Plain base fabric
- One 6½ × 6½in (16.5 × 16.5cm) equilateral triangle

Calico lining
- 8⅜ × 15⅝in (21 × 39cm) rectangle

Fabric scraps
- Twelve 3½in (8.9cm) equilateral triangles in various fabrics, both plain and patterned

FINISHED SIZE

6 × 6 × 6in (15.2 × 15.2 × 15.2cm)

METHOD

To stitch the EPP

1 Cut out and tack (baste) all your EPPs. Lay the smaller triangles out as indicated on the layout to make a pattern you like.

2 Join the small triangles together with whip stitch (page 20). Give your work a good press with a hot iron. Remove the papers from any triangles that you have whip stitched round all three sides.

3 Take your 6in (15.2cm) equilateral triangle and stitch it to the edge of the main piece as shown, using whip stitch.

To finish the door stop

4 Folding your work, join edge B to edge C with whip stitch. Next, join edge A to edge D. Then join edge E to edge F. When joining edges E and F, leave a 3in (7.6cm) gap unstitched at the centre of this edge for turning and filling later. As you work, carefully take your papers out by snipping the thread. You will find it easier to sew the shapes accurately if you leave the paper in while you work. Turn your work right sides out through the gap left open on edge E/F.

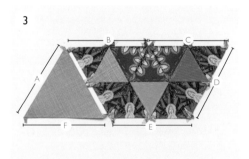

5 Fold the raw edges of your pyramid's turning gap in by their ¼in (0.65cm) seam allowance and tack. Fold your lining fabric in half to form a square, aligning the raw edges. Stitch a ⅜in (1cm) seam but remember to leave a 2½in (6.3cm) gap at one corner for turning and filling.

6 Turn your lining square right sides out and push into the EPP pyramid, leaving the filling opening protruding from the opening in the pyramid.

7 Fill with rice or lentils with a teaspoon (or by fashioning a funnel by rolling up a sheet of paper) through the turning gap until you have your required density and weight. Don't over-fill; leave about 1in (2.5cm) empty at the top of the lining.

8 Close the turning gap with small, close whip stitch and remove the tacking.

5

6

7

8

CHRISTMAS DECORATION

DESIGNED BY JEMIMA SCHLEE

Make a sweet little star to adorn your Christmas tree top or hang in a window over the holidays. How special, to hand-make a decoration that will last a lifetime and become an heirloom. Re-scale this project to make small 'baubles' or make some as a very personal decoration to tie to a gift for loved ones, relatives or friends.

SKILL LEVEL: BEGINNER

YOU'LL NEED

Templates
- Twenty-four 2in (5cm) paper equilateral triangles (page 139)

Fabric
- Fabric scraps in turquoise plain or patterned fabrics in three different complementary patterns

Haberdashery
- 6in (15.2cm) narrow white rickrack or narrow white ribbon
- Two small white buttons
- White thread
- Thread to match your fabrics
- Scissors, needle, pins
- Rotary cutter, ruler and mat (optional)
- Sewing machine (optional)

CUTTING

Patterned fabric scraps
- Twenty-four 2½in (6.3cm) equilateral triangles

FINISHED SIZE

6½ × 6½in (16.5 × 16.5 cm)

METHOD

To stitch the EPP

1 Cut out and tack (baste) all your EPPs. Lay them out in order, creating two stars, before piecing them together individually and sewing together with whip stitch (page 20).

2 Leave one seam of one star unstitched to create your turning gap. Place the two EPPs right sides together and stitch all around the outside edges.

To finish the decoration

3 Carefully take your papers out. Turn your work right sides out very gently through the small turning gap.

4 Gently take your time to tease and tweak the outside edges to make them sharp. Use a needle to pick carefully at the tips of the six points. Give your work a good press with a hot iron. Slip stitch (page 24) the opening closed.

5 Fold your rickrack or ribbon in half and attach to either side of one point 'sandwiched' by the two small buttons.

1

2

3

4

5
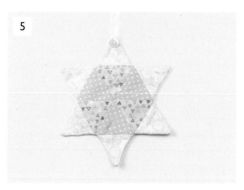

PROJECTS USING
CLAMSHELLS

HOT WATER BOTTLE COVER

DESIGNED BY JANET GODDARD

There is nothing better on a cold evening than to snuggle up with a hot water bottle. This cover features clamshell EPP in bright, cheerful fabrics, it is softly padded to make it super-comforting and it will fit most hot water bottles. It will make a perfect gift for anyone who feels the cold.

SKILL LEVEL: CONFIDENT

YOU'LL NEED

Templates
- Twenty-one 3½in (8.9cm) paper clamshells (page 139)

Fabric
Requirements based on fabrics with a useable width of 42in (107cm)
- 12in (30.5cm) grey for the front and back
- 12in (30.5cm) mustard print for the lining
- Fabric scraps in pink, blue, green, mustard and white for the clamshells

Haberdashery
- 12in (30.5cm) fusible wadding (batting)
- 40in (1m) blue ribbon, 1in (2.5cm) wide
- Pale grey thread for piecing and quilting
- Scissors, needle, pins
- Rotary cutter, ruler and mat (optional)
- Sewing machine

CUTTING

Grey fabric
- Two 15½ × 10½in (39.4 × 26.7cm) rectangles

Mustard print fabric
- Two 15½ × 10½in (39.4 × 26.7cm) rectangles

Fabric scraps
- Twenty-one clamshells

Fusible wadding (batting)
- Two 15½ × 10½in (39.4 × 26.7cm) rectangles

FINISHED SIZE

10 × 15in (25 × 38.1cm)

METHOD

To stitch the EPP

1 The preparation of these clamshell shapes is slightly different from that of other EPP shapes. The fabric is folded over the curved top edge of the clamshell and tacked (basted) in place. The remaining fabric is not folded over the shape. The bottom of the fabric is cut in line with the point of the template.

2 Take one grey rectangle and measure 5in (12.7cm) down from the top of a 10½in (26.7cm) edge. Draw a line or place a ruler there to mark the measurement. Take three prepared clamshells and pin on to the rectangle, ensuring that the top of each clamshell touches the line.

3 Slip stitch (page 24) the clamshells in place by stitching the folded curved edge of each shape. Press and remove the papers.

4 Take four prepared clamshells and position these in place in between each of the clamshells in row one. These clamshells need to overlap the raw edges of the top row of clamshells by ¼in (0.65cm). Pin and stitch the clamshells in place. Press and remove the papers. Continue in this way, repeating the process to create six rows in total.

To finish the hot water bottle cover

5 Trim the overhanging clamshells in line with the sides and bottom of the grey rectangle.

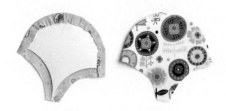

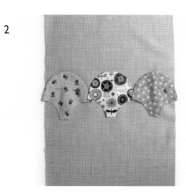

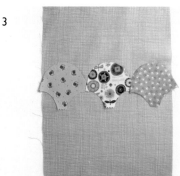

6 Iron the fusible wadding (batting) to the wrong side of both grey rectangles. Using the grey thread, quilt (page 23) vertical lines from top to bottom through both the fabric and the wadding (batting) at 2in (5cm) intervals.

7 Fold the ribbon in half and place it on the right side of the plain grey rectangle, in the middle, 3½in (8.9cm) from the top raw edge. Pin in place and stitch down with one vertical line of machine or back stitching.

8 Place the two quilted units right sides together and machine stitch up each long side and across the bottom. Trim the corners and turn through. To stitch the lining, repeat with the two 15½ × 10½in (39.4 × 26.7cm) mustard rectangles, leaving a 4in (10cm) gap in stitching in the middle of one side. Trim the corners.

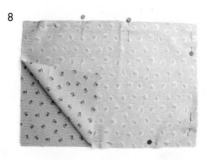

9 Place the outer hot water bottle cover inside the lining, right sides together, and pin all the way around the top edge. Machine stitch around the edge, matching the side seams.

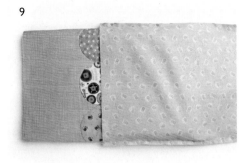

10 Turn the hot water bottle cover right side out through the opening in the lining and stitch the opening closed with neat slip stitches. Carefully press the top of the hot water bottle cover so that ¼in (0.65cm) of the lining is showing on the outside and pin in place. Stitch through the layers in the seam line around the top.

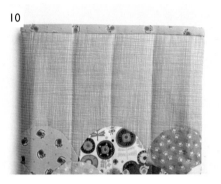

11 Place the hot water bottle inside the cover and tie the ribbon with a neat bow.

Tips
The cover fits a hot water bottle measuring 8 × 13in (20.3 × 33cm), however there is room within the cover for a slightly larger or smaller hot water bottle.

After stitching the ribbon to the outer section, fold it up and pin it to the grey fabric before stitching the units together. This will ensure that the ribbon doesn't get caught into the stitching.

CLAMSHELL CUSHION

DESIGNED BY JANET GODDARD

A vibrant and fun cushion featuring a clamshell design where the pool party inspired fabrics sit against an aqua background. The cushion is softly quilted and finished with an envelope back.

SKILL LEVEL: CONFIDENT

YOU'LL NEED

Templates
- Eighteen 3½in (8.9cm) paper clamshells (page 139)

Fabric
Requirements based on fabrics with a useable width of 42in (107cm)
- 20in (50.4cm) aqua for the cushion front and envelope back
- 4in (10cm) blue print for the outer border
- 18in (45.7cm) cream for the inner backing
- Fabric scraps in pink, blue, green, yellow and white for the clamshells

Haberdashery
- 18in (45.7cm) wadding (batting)
- Pale grey thread for piecing and quilting
- 16in (40.6cm) cushion pad
- Scissors, needle, pins
- Rotary cutter, ruler and mat (optional)
- Sewing machine

CUTTING

Aqua fabric
- One 14½ × 14½in (36.8 × 36.8cm) square
- Two 17½ × 12in (44.5 × 30.5cm) rectangles

Blue print
- Two 2 × 14½in (5 × 36.8cm) strips
- Two 2 × 17½in (5 × 44.5cm) strips

Cream fabric
- One 18 × 18in (45.7 × 45.7cm) square

Fabric scraps
- Eighteen clamshells

FINISHED SIZE

17 × 17in (43.2 × 43.2cm)

METHOD

To stitch the EPP

1 The preparation of these clamshell shapes is slightly different from that of other EPP shapes. The fabric is folded over the curved top edge of the clamshell and tacked (basted) in place. The remaining fabric is not folded over the shape. The bottom of the fabric is cut in line with the point of the template.

2 Take the aqua square and measure 7in (17.8cm) down from the top. Draw a line or place a ruler there to mark the measurement. Take four prepared clamshells and pin on to the square, ensuring that the top of each clamshell touches the line.

3 Slip stitch (page 24) the clamshells in place by stitching the folded curved edge of each shape. Press and remove the papers.

4 Take five prepared clamshells and position these in place in between each of the clamshells in row one. These clamshells need to overlap the raw edges of the top row of clamshells by ¼in (0.65cm)

5 Pin and slip stitch the clamshells in place. Press and remove the papers. Continue in this way, repeating the process for four rows in total.

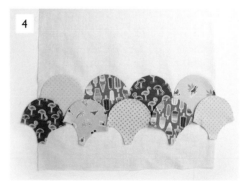

To finish the cushion

6 Trim the overhanging clamshells in line with the sides and bottom of the aqua square.

7 Take the two 2 × 14½in (5 × 36.8cm) blue print strips and stitch to the top and bottom of the cushion front. Press the seams away from the middle. Take the two 2 × 17½in (5 × 44.5cm) blue print strips and stitch to the sides of the cushion front. Press the seams away from the middle.

8 Layer the cushion top by placing the cream square wrong side up on a surface, followed by the wadding (batting) and then the cushion top, centrally and right side up. Secure with pins. Machine quilt (page 23) ½in (1.3cm) away from the curved edges of the clamshells on the top row and then in the ditch (page 24) of the curved top of the clamshells on the remaining rows. Stitch in the ditch between the aqua square and the blue print border.

9 Trim the wadding and backing in line with the cushion top. To prepare the envelope back for the cushion, take the two 17½ × 12in (44.5 × 30.5cm) aqua rectangles and on one 17½in (44.5cm) edge of each, fold and press ¼in (0.65cm) towards the wrong side. Stitch. On one of the rectangles, fold the edge again by 2in (5cm) to create a hem, press, pin and stitch the hem. Place the rectangle with the double folded edge, right side facing the cushion front with the folded edge in the middle and then the second rectangle on top so that the folded edges in the middle overlap. Pin around the outer edge.

10 Machine stitch around the outer edge of the cushion. Trim the corners and turn through so that the right side is facing out. Press well.

11 Insert the cushion pad.

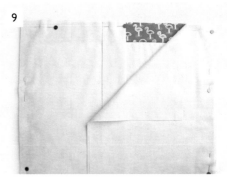

Tips
If you are short of time you could omit the quilting stage, leaving out the cream fabric and wadding (batting).

I have used coordinating fabric scraps from a single range of fabrics, however this project would work well with a mix of fabric scraps.

PROJECTS USING APPLE CORES

TOTE BAG

DESIGNED BY JEMIMA SCHLEE

A decorative tote bag appliquéd with floral 'windmills' made using apple core EPPs. These instructions include how to make your own bag, but you could also dress up an existing bag, covering any printed logos with your appliquéd swirls. This is another great project for using up little scraps of fabric.

SKILL LEVEL: CONFIDENT

YOU'LL NEED

Templates

- Sixteen 3in (7.6cm) paper apple cores (page 140)

Fabric

Requirements based on fabrics with a useable width of 42in (107cm)

- 22in (56cm) orange linen or cotton
- Fabric scraps in turquoise, turquoise pattern, beige pattern and pink pattern for the windmills for each side of your bag

Haberdashery

- White thread
- Threads to match your fabrics
- Quilting needle and quilting thread
- Scissors, needle, pins
- Rotary cutter, ruler and mat (optional)
- Safety pin
- Sewing machine

CUTTING

Orange fabric

- One 32 × 14½in (81.2 × 36.8cm) rectangle for the body of your bag
- Two 36 × 3in (91 × 7.6cm) strips for the handles

Fabric scraps

- Eight 4½in (11.4cm) apple core pieces for one side, sixteen if you are decorating both sides, cut on the bias

FINISHED SIZE

13 × 16in (33 × 40.6cm) bag;
15in (38.1cm) handles

METHOD

To stitch the EPP

1 When you tack (baste) your fabric shapes to the 3in (7.6cm) paper pieces, pin them first as however confident you are as this is quite a fiddly shape. Remember to cut the shapes on the bias. Make sure you make quite small tacking stitches along these paper pieces to avoid pleats and wrinkles gathering along the convex edges, snipping the seam allowance carefully along concave edges (page 24).

2 Stitch your pieces together in groups of four. Press with a hot iron. Carefully take your papers out by snipping the thread. Take great care to keep the convex and concave edges along the outside circumference folded under ¼in (0.65cm) and re-tack along their edges. Give your work a good press with a hot iron.

To make and finish your tote bag

3 Fold one strip of linen in half along its long axis, creating a 1½in (3.8cm) wide strip. Pin or tack (baste) the long raw edges together before sewing a ⅜in (1cm) seam along it.

4 Remove the pins or tacking. Use your safety pin to pull one end of your strip through the channel you have created and out of the other end to leave it right side out.

5 Tweak the seam along your strip to make it sharp before giving it a good press. Top stitch (page 24) along both sides of your handle ⅛in (0.32cm) from the edges.

1
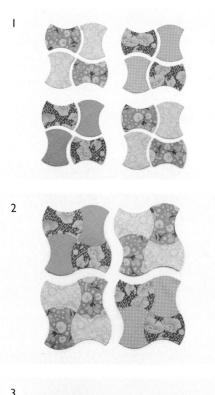

2

3

4

5

6 Lay your large piece of bag fabric down in front of you (wrong way up if it has a front and back). Fold in half along its short axis and align the edges to make a 16 × 14½in (40.6 × 36.8cm) rectangle. Make French seams along the sides of your bag to avoid them fraying with use. To do this, pin or tack the two long edges, wrong sides together. Stitch a ⅜in (1cm) seam down each of the tacked edges at 45 degrees. Trim the seam allowance to ¼in (0.65cm) and snip the two bottom corners at 45 degrees.

7 Turn your work wrong side out. Tweak and tease the seams to make them sharp before giving them a good press. Pin or tack along these two pressed seams.

8 Stitch a ⅜in (1cm) seam along each side seam, fully enclosing the raw edges.

9 With your work still inside out, fold down the top open raw edge of your bag by 1in (2.5cm) and press.

10 Fold this edge over once more by another 1in (2.5cm) and press. Pin in place. Mark a point at the middle of the top of each side of your bag. Taking one handle at a time, push the raw ends under the hem to fit snugly into the pressed fold positioned 3in (7.6cm) either side of the middle pins. Make sure your handles are not twisted.

6

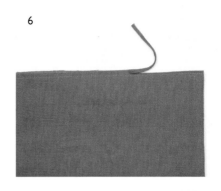

7

8

9

10

11 Stitch along the hem ¹⁄₁₆in (0.16cm) from the edge. With your work still inside out, fold the handles up to their final position and pin in place.

12 Turn your work right sides out and top stitch along the top ¹⁄₁₆in (0.16cm) from the edge, reverse stitching as you pass each handle end for extra strength.

13 Fold your bag in half and press it to create a crease from between the two handles to the middle of the bottom. Position two of your windmills centred along this line – the first one 2in (5cm) from the top edge, the top tip of the second just touching the bottom tip of the first. Pin or tack into position.

14 Stitch your EPP on to your bag with small hemming stitches around their circumferences before quilting (page 23) just inside their edges.

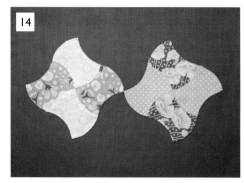

APPLE CORE CUSHION

DESIGNED BY JEMIMA SCHLEE

Rich vibrant fabrics and mixed patterns make up this striking rectangular cushion, a great shape on a sofa or occasional chair where a larger cushion would dominate. The juxtaposition of fabrics in this design makes an eclectic addition when grouped with any mix of cushion shapes and colours. It's a great project for using up scraps, and the design can be easily adjusted to a square format.

SKILL LEVEL: CONFIDENT

YOU'LL NEED

Templates
- Twelve 4in (10cm) paper apple cores (page 140)

Fabric
Requirements based on fabrics with a useable width of 42in (107cm)
- 14in (35.6cm) turquoise floral fabric for front and back button flap
- 14in (35.6cm) purple print for back panel
- Fabric scraps of turquoise pattern and blue pattern, or two contrasting fabrics, for the apple cores

Haberdashery
- Three buttons, ⅝in (1.6cm) diameter
- 20½ × 12½in (52 × 31.8cm) cushion pad (being slightly larger than your cushion cover, this produces a good, snug fit when you finish)
- White thread
- Thread to match your fabrics
- Scissors, needle, pins
- Rotary cutter, ruler and mat (optional)
- Sewing machine

CUTTING

Turquoise floral fabric
- One 19¾ × 11¾in (50 × 30cm) rectangle for cushion front, this includes a ⅜in (1cm) seam allowance
- One 8 × 11¾in (20.3 × 30cm) rectangle

Purple print fabric
- One 19¾ × 11¾in (50 × 30cm) rectangle, this includes a ⅜in (1cm) seam allowance

Purple patterned fabric scraps
- Six 4½in (11.4cm) apple cores in purple pattern, cut on the bias

Turquoise patterned fabric scraps
- Six 4½in (11.4cm) apple cores in turquoise pattern, cut on the bias

FINISHED SIZE

19 × 11¼in (48.2 × 28.6cm)

METHOD

To stitch the EPP

1 Cut out your fabric for your apple cores on the bias to avoid puckering and wrinkles. Make sure you make quite small tacking (basting) stitches along these paper pieces to avoid pleats and wrinkles along the curved contours; you can use gathering on the projecting convex curves. Clip the seam allowance on the concave curves (page 24). Lay your pieces out in position.

2 Take two of your pieces, one in each pattern, and whip stitch (page 20) the convex curve of one to the concave curve of its neighbour. Continue in this fashion, following the layout chart, until your pieces are all stitched together. Give your work a press with a hot iron.

3 Carefully take your papers out by snipping the thread. Give your work a good press with a hot iron, keeping the folds on one long edge and pressing the folds open along the other three edges. Try hard not to stretch the edges of the fabric – if your sewing machine is right there, you can top stitch (page 24) very close to the edge to ensure this.

To finish the cushion

4 Lay down your front fabric rectangle right side up and place your EPP front right side up on top of it and aligned with the right-hand edge. The curved edges of some EPP will protrude over the base fabric's edge. Press again before pinning around the edges. Tack (baste) the two layers of fabric together using tacking from the centre of your work out to the edges in a sunray pattern, smoothing out the fabric as you go to minimize wrinkles. Top stitch by hand along the edge where the EPP meets the base fabric.

5 Prepare your two pieces of fabric for the backing. Take your largest piece of backing (purple) and, with the wrong side facing you, fold one short edge in by 1¼in (3.2cm). Press with a hot iron and fold over 1¼in (3.2cm) once more. Press with a hot iron before sewing this hem by machine using the matching thread. Hem one short edge of the other backing piece (turquoise) in the same way.

6 Make three buttonholes perpendicular to and starting 5/8in (1.6cm) in from the folded hem edge. Place one centrally and the other two 2½in (6.3cm) to either side of this as shown on the photograph.

7 Lay the two backing pieces down in front of you, right side up and the hemmed edge of the larger piece overlapping the hemmed edge of the smaller piece so that the button holes are on the top layer. Place your cushion front on top, right side up, and align all the raw edges. You may need to adjust the overlap of the backing pieces so that the short edges all match. Pin and then tack the front and backing fabrics together around the edges.

8 Machine stitch ⅜in (1cm) seams all the way around. Reverse stitch over the multiple layers of fabric above and below where the back pieces overlap to give these points extra strength. Zigzag stitch around all four raw seam edges.

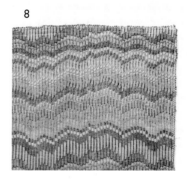

9 Turn your work right side out. Prod the corners gently from inside to make them as sharp as you can. There is no need to snip the excess fabric off the corners at 45 degrees as this extra bulk will fill where the cushion pad does not quite reach. Give it another good press and sew on the three buttons to correspond with the buttonholes. Stuff your cover with your cushion pad.

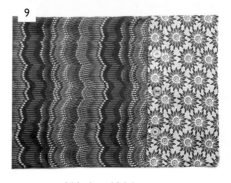

PROJECTS
COMBINING SHAPES

BUTTON BAG

DESIGNED BY JEMIMA SCHLEE

This is a simple drawstring bag for corralling your button collection, so I've decorated it with stylized buttons made from pentagons, but you could choose different shapes. Add as many shapes as you like – I put a single one on the back at the last minute. Reassign it as a scrabble tile bag by using square templates embroidered with letters.

SKILL LEVEL: CONFIDENT

YOU'LL NEED

Templates
- Five (or six) 1½in (3.8cm) paper pentagons (page 138)

Fabric
Requirements based on fabrics with a useable width of 42in (107cm)
- 12in (30.5cm) plain (or textured) teal fabric for bag outer
- 12in (30.5cm) patterned turquoise fabric for lining
- Fabric scraps in pink pattern, plain dark pink, terracotta and burgundy for the pentagons

Haberdashery
- 28in (71cm) bias binding for drawstring
- White thread
- Thread to match your fabrics
- Black buttonhole thread or fine embroidery thread
- Scissors, needle, pins
- Rotary cutter, ruler and mat (optional)
- Sewing machine
- Safety pin
- Seam ripper (optional)

CUTTING

Teal fabric
- One 19 × 21¼in (48.2 × 54cm) rectangle for outer, this includes a ⅜in (1cm) seam allowance

Patterned turquoise fabric
- One 19 × 21¼in (48.2 × 54cm) rectangle for outer, this includes a ⅜in (1cm) seam allowance

Fabric scraps
- Five (or six) × 2in (5cm) pentagons

FINISHED SIZE

9¼ × 10in (23.5 × 25cm)

METHOD

To stitch the EPP

1 Cut out and tack (baste) all your EPPs. Lay them out in order before piecing them together with a whip stitch (page 20).

2 Carefully take your papers out. Give your work a good press with a hot iron, pressing the outside edges and their seam allowance still folded in. Try hard not to stretch the edges of the fabric.

To finish the button bag

3 Position your pentagonal 'buttons' on your bag fabric, 2⅛in (5.5cm) from the bottom edge of the fabric and 2⅛in (5.5cm) from the left-hand edge. Pin or tack in position. Stitch your pentagons on carefully by hand.

4 Add embroidery following the image as a guide. Use thick buttonhole thread, thin embroidery thread, or simply double up normal embroidery thread. For the 'holes', simply make four stitches about ⅜in (1cm) long and fanned over each other. Remove any pins or tacking.

5 Press your work with a hot iron. With your work lying right side up in front of you and the 'buttons' nearest you, lay the lining fabric right side down on top of it and align all the raw side edges. Pin or tack along the top edge before machine stitching a ⅜in (1cm) seam along this edge.

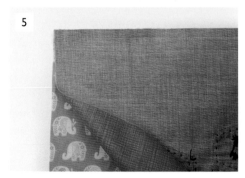

6 Remove any pins or tacking. Press your seam to the lining side of your work with a hot iron. Fold your work in half along its long axis – outside fabric onto outside fabric, lining onto lining – and align all the raw edges. Pin or tack around your work, leaving a 3in (7.6cm) gap in stitching in the lining seam for turning it the right way out, and a drawstring channel opening starting about 1⅜in (4cm) from the top edge of the outside fabric, finishing about 2in (5cm) from the top edge. Machine stitch a ⅜in (1cm) seam all the way round, remembering to reverse stitch at either side of both the drawstring channel opening and the turning gap.

7 Remove any pins or tacking and turn your work right sides out through the turning gap.

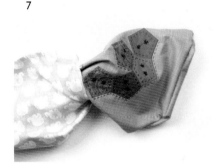

8 Press the side seam with the drawstring channel open. Use your black thread to make small running stitches (around the gap to keep it open. Turn the raw edges in at the turning gap by ⅜in (1cm) and close with a neat slip stitch (page 24).

9 Push your lining down into your bag's outer, prodding the two bottom corners from the inside to make them as sharp as you can. Give your work a good press, ensuring the top edge where the outer meets the lining is sharp and crisp. Tack around the top edge, and again 1⅜in (4cm) from the top edge, another 2in (5cm) from the top edge, this is to form the drawstring channel making sure the opening is between the two lines of stitches. Use your machine to top stitch ⅛in (0.32cm) in from the top edge and again along both tacked drawstring channels. Remove all the tacking.

10 Fold your bias binding in half along its long axis and press with a hot iron. Use matching thread on your machine to top stitch ⅛in (0.32cm) down the edge of the binding to create a drawstring.

11 Use the safety pin to run your drawstring through its channel. Finish by tying a simple knot at each end of the drawstring to prevent it disappearing into the channel in use.

NEEDLE CASE

DESIGNED BY JEMIMA SCHLEE

I've always used a needle book to keep my mismatched collection of needles together. The odd pin and safety pin can be stored here too, and arranging the contents neatly now and again is incredibly satisfying. The outer is pieced squares and rectangles that are quilted in simple graphic circles. Its four felt pages are edged using pinking shears, making them extra cute.

SKILL LEVEL: CONFIDENT

YOU'LL NEED

Templates
- Four 2in (5cm) paper squares (page 140)
- Eight 1 × 2in (2.5 × 5cm) paper rectangles (page 140)

Fabric
Requirements based on fabrics with a useable width of 42in (107cm)
- 6in (15.2cm) fabric for lining
- 8in (20.3cm) square felt
- Fabric scraps in three colours for squares and rectangles

Haberdashery
- 9in (23cm) wadding (batting)
- 29in (73.6cm) bias binding
- White thread
- Thread to match your fabrics
- Scissors, needle, pins
- Rotary cutter, ruler and mat (optional)
- Sewing machine (optional)
- Pinking shears (optional)
- Seam ripper (optional)

CUTTING

Lining fabric
- 9 × 5in (23 × 12.7cm) rectangle

Felt
- 4 × 8in (10 × 20.3cm)

Plain fabric scraps
- Four 2½in (6.3cm) squares in dark fabric
- Four 1½ × 2½in (3.8 × 6.3cm) rectangles in medium fabric

Patterned fabric scraps
- Four 1½ × 2½in (3.8 × 6.3cm) rectangles in light fabric

Wadding (batting)
- 9 × 5in (23 × 12.7cm) rectangle for interlining, this includes ¼in (0.65cm) seam allowance

FINISHED SIZE

4¼ × 4½in (10.8 × 11.4cm)

METHOD

To stitch the EPP

1 Cut out and tack (baste) all your EPPs. Lay them out in order.

2 Stitch your pieces together with whip stitch (page 20) and give your work a press with a hot iron.

3 Carefully take out your papers. Give your work another good press with a hot iron, this time opening out the seam allowance on all four outside edges.

To finish the needle case

4 Lay your lining fabric right side down and lay your wadding centrally on top of it. Now place your EPP on top and smooth the layers with your hand or an iron to minimize any wrinkles. Pin or baste the layers together before quilting circles (page 23) on each square and centred on each pair of rectangles – eight in all. Trim off any excess lining and wadding (batting) flush with the ¼in (0.65cm) seam allowance of your pieced work.

5 Bind your four edges with straight or bias binding (page 23), folding the corners neatly.

6 Use pinking shears to trim the edge of your felt. With your work in front of you, lining facing up, lay the felt down to fit just within the border of bias binding. Pin in place.

7 Stitch through all layers to attach the felt to the spine of your little fabric book. Work slowly from both sides to get your stitches even on the inside, and lost in the stitches between EPPs on the outside (page 24).

6

7

PIN CUSHION

DESIGNED BY JEMIMA SCHLEE

Pin cushions are so useful, not just for storing your pins and needles, but for collecting up your pins safely as you remove them from your work. This project is made from squares and triangles, so if you like complete order you can use the EPP area colours to house different needles and pins. This pretty pin cushion is a sewing necessity that also makes a good gift and, in time, can become a family heirloom.

SKILL LEVEL: BEGINNER

YOU'LL NEED

Templates
- One 2in (5cm) paper square (page 139)
- Twelve 2in (5cm) paper equilateral triangles (page 139)
- One 4in (10cm) paper square (page 139)

Fabric
Requirements based on fabrics with a useable width of 42in (107cm)
- 4½in (11.4cm) orange for the base
- Fabric scraps in purple, turquoise and orange for the pin cushion top

Haberdashery
- White thread
- Thread to match your fabrics
- Two good handfuls of hollow fibre stuffing – more if you want your pin cushion to be very firm
- Scissors, needle, pins
- Rotary cutter, ruler and mat (optional)
- Sewing machine (optional)

CUTTING

Orange base fabric
- One 4½in (11.4cm) square

Patterned fabric scraps
- One 2½in (6.3cm) square
- Twelve 2½in (6.3cm) equilateral triangles

FINISHED SIZE

1½ × 4 × 4in (3.8 × 10 × 10cm)

METHOD

To stitch the EPP

1 Cut out and tack (baste) all your EPP pieces and lay them down following the design layout.

2 Follow the layout to piece your EPPs together with whip stitch (page 20) to produce a dome-shaped piece of patchwork. With your work inside out, stitch the base square to the four edges of your dome, leaving a 2in (5cm) turning gap in the centre of one edge.

To finish the pin cushion

3 Remove your EPP papers carefully. Give your work a press with a hot iron. Take out the papers from any shape that has all its sides joined to another shape. Turn your work right sides out through the turning gap and gently prod the four corners to make them as sharp as you can without stretching the hand stitching.

4 Fill with hollow fibre through the turning gap until you have your required density of stuffing. Fold the raw edges of the turning gap by their ¼in (0.65cm) seam allowance and tack in place.

Finish your work off by closing the turning gap with small hand slip stitches (page 24).

1

2

3

4

PENTAGON BALL
DESIGNED BY JEMIMA SCHLEE

Very pretty and simple to make, this is great for using up scraps and so easy to re-scale. You could make a rattle by stuffing a couple of 'jingle' bells in with the stuffing. Make six large and one small ball to make an indoor set of boules. Alternatively, you could fill with dried lentils or beans to make a door stop or paper weight. Stitch a little ribbon loop to the top to make a decoration or Christmas bauble.

SKILL LEVEL: BEGINNER

YOU'LL NEED

Templates
- Twelve 1½in (3.8cm) paper pentagons (page 140)

Fabric
- Fabric scraps in different colours and patterns

Haberdashery
- Hollow fibre stuffing
- White thread
- Sewing thread to match your fabrics
- Scissors, needle, pins
- Rotary cutter, ruler and mat (optional)
- Sewing machine (optional)
- Seam ripper (optional)

CUTTING

Fabric scraps
- Twelve 2in (5cm) pentagons

FINISHED SIZE

5in (12.7cm) diameter

METHOD

To stitch the EPP

1 Cut out and tack (baste) your pentagons. Lay them out in position to work from.

2 Take two of your pieces from one set of six EPPs and whip stitch (page 20) two edges together. Continue in this fashion until you have all six pieces stitched together. Repeat this with the second set of six pentagons – you will now have two half spheres.

3 Now join the two hemispheres together, leaving the final seam open for a turning gap. Carefully take your papers out by snipping the thread from any shape that has all its sides joined to another shape. Turn your work right side out through the turning gap.

To finish the ball

4 Fold the seam allowance in around the turning gap and tack in place. Stuff your work with hollow fibre, adding a bell at this point if you wish.

5 Close the turning gap with small, neat slip stitches (page 24).

> *Tip*
> You can also make balls with six segments, like the one in the photo on page 2.

GLASSES CASE

DESIGNED BY JANET GODDARD

This padded glasses case is ideal for either sun glasses or everyday glasses and will slip easily into a bag when you are out and about. Embellished with a flower motif and softly padded with wadding (batting), the case will provide great protection for your glasses.

SKILL LEVEL: CONFIDENT

YOU'LL NEED

Templates
- Eight 1¼in (3.2cm) paper petals (page 140)
- One 1in (2.5cm) diameter paper circle (page 140)

Fabric
Requirements based on fabrics with a useable width of 42in (107cm)
- 5in (12.7cm) grey for the case outer
- 5in (12.7cm) green for the case lining and petals
- Fabric scraps in pink and pink floral for the centre circle and petals

Haberdashery
- 5in (12.7cm) fusible wadding (batting)
- Grey thread for piecing
- Green embroidery thread for quilting
- 4in (10cm) strip of thin elastic
- One button, ½in (1.3cm) diameter
- Scissors, needle, pins
- Rotary cutter, ruler and mat (optional)
- Sewing machine

CUTTING

Grey fabric
- One 5 × 19in (12.7 × 48.2cm) rectangle

Green fabric
- One 5 × 19in (12.7 × 48.2cm) rectangle
- Four petals

Fabric scraps
- Four pink floral petals
- One pink circle

Fusible wadding (batting)
- One 5 × 19in (12.7 × 48.2cm) rectangle

FINISHED SIZE

8 × 4½in (20.3 × 11.4cm)

METHOD

To stitch the EPP

1 Cut out and tack (baste) the eight petals and lay them out into a circular design, alternating the green and pink floral colours.

2 Whip stitch (page 20) the eight petals together by stitching one side of each petal to another until all eight are stitched together in a circle.

To finish the glasses case

3 Press and remove the papers from the petals. Remove the paper from the circle and slip stitch (page 24) it to the middle of the circle of petals. Take the grey rectangle and fold it in half so that the short sides are meeting. Press the fold line to get a crease, then reopen the rectangle. Measure up 1½in (3.8cm) from the creased line on the right side of the fabric and slip stitch the flower in place.

4 Iron the fusible wadding (batting) to the wrong side of the grey rectangle completed in step 3.

5 Using the green embroidery thread, quilt (page 23) around the flower shape ¼in (0.65cm) from the outer edge of the petals.

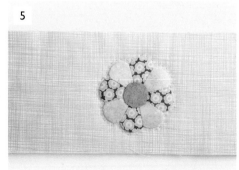

6 Take the 4in (10cm) strip of elastic, fold in half and stitch the raw ends to the middle of the short edge of the grey rectangle that is at the opposite end to that of the flower. Use an ⅛in (0.32cm) seam.

7 With right sides together, fold the grey rectangle in half so that the short sides are open at the top, then stitch down each side. Repeat with the green rectangle but leave a 2in (5cm) gap in the stitching on one long side. Trim the corners.

8 Turn the grey rectangle so that it is right side out, then put it inside the green rectangle so that the right side of the outer case is facing the right side of the lining. Pin and stitch around the top.

9 Turn the case through the gap so it is right side out. Press carefully and slip stitch to close the gap in the lining. Stitch the button 1in (2.5cm) above the flower, being careful to only stitch through the upper side of the case. Loop the elastic around the button to create a folded top.

Tip
Although this glasses case fits a standard size pair of glasses, different styles of glasses vary in shape and size so the pattern may need adjusting to fit. When measuring the glasses remember to allow for wadding (batting).

DRAWSTRING BAG
DESIGNED BY JEMIMA SCHLEE

A bold drawstring bag makes the dullest item sing. It can be used for a myriad of things, and the choice of colours and fabric can reflect its use or its user. This is a project that can be easily re-scaled – a small bag for precious jewellery, a large one for laundry, and so many other uses in between. If you're making this as a gift, have fun with the drawstring ends – add pom-poms, bells, tassels or whatever takes your fancy.

SKILL LEVEL: CONFIDENT

YOU'LL NEED

Templates
- Two 3in (7.6cm) paper squares (page 138)
- Eight 3in (7.6cm) paper eight-point diamonds (page 138)
- Eight 2⅛in (5.3cm) paper half-square triangles (page 138)

Fabric
Requirements based on fabrics with a useable width of 42in (107cm)

Plain calico is not usually pre-shrunk so wash, iron and press it before cutting if you are using calico as I did.

- 12in (30.5cm) plain dark grey fabric for the outer
- 20in (50.4cm) calico for the outer, lining and drawstrings
- Fabric scraps in various colours and patterns for the shapes

Haberdashery
- White thread
- Threads to match your fabrics
- Scissors, needle, pins
- Rotary cutter, ruler and mat (optional)
- Safety pin
- Sewing machine
- Seam ripper (optional)

CUTTING

Grey outer fabric

- Two 10½ × 5½in (26.7 × 14cm) rectangles of calico for bag outer (upper), this includes a ¼in (0.65cm) seam allowance
- Two 10½ × 5¾ (26.6 × 14.6cm) rectangles of dark fabric for bag outer (lower), this includes a ¼in (0.65cm) seam allowance

Lining fabric

- One 10½ × 29½in (26.7 × 75cm) rectangle of calico for bag lining, this includes a ¼in (0.65cm) seam allowance
- Two 30 × 1½in (76 × 3.8cm) strips of calico for the drawstrings, this includes a ⅜in (1cm) seam allowance

Patterned fabric scraps

- Eight 3½in (8.9cm) paper eight-point diamonds, four in each of two colours

Plain fabric scraps

- Two 3½in (8.9cm) squares
- Eight 2⅝in (6.7cm) half-square triangles

FINISHED SIZE

10 × 14½in (25 × 36.8cm)

METHOD

To stitch the EPPs

1 Tack (baste) all the EPPs. Stitch them together using whip stitch (page 20) following the layout to create two finished EPP pieces.

2 When you have completed your piecing, give your two pieces of work a good press.

To finish the drawstring bag

3 Carefully remove the paper. Press the raw selvedge around the edges of both EPP pieces out. Trim off the tail ends of fabric extending past the selvedge edges. Working on one side of your bag at a time, take one of the dark 'lower' rectangles and place right side up in front of you. Place one EPP right side down on top of it. Align both their top long edges. Pin or tack in place. Stitch a ¼in (0.65cm) seam along this edge.

4 Press the seam to the grey fabric side with a hot iron.

5 Turn your work 180 degrees and repeat this process with one 'upper' calico rectangle. This is one side of your outer completed. Use your machine to top stitch (page 24) ⅛in (0.32cm) either side of each EPP on the calico and dark fabric sides.

1

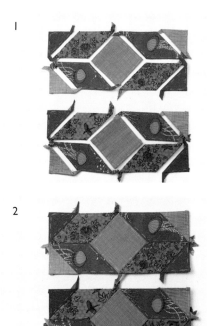

2

3

4

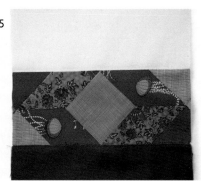

5

6 Repeat steps 3 to 5 to complete the second side. Place the two outer pieces right sides together and stitch a ¼in (0.65cm) seam along the bottom dark raw edges. Press this seam open and lay it right side up in front of you. Lay the lining fabric right side down on top of it and align all the raw edges. Pin or tack along the two short edges at either end before machine stitching a seam along them.

7 Remove the pins or tacking. Press the seams to the lining side of your work with a hot iron. Re-fold your work – outside fabric onto outside fabric, lining onto lining – and align two long raw side edges. Pin or tack around your work, leaving a 3in (7.6cm) gap in stitching in the lining seam for turning it the right way out, and a drawstring channel opening on each side starting about 1½in (3.8cm) from the top edge of the outside fabric, finishing about 2½in (6.3cm) from the top edge. Machine stitch both the side seams, remembering to reverse stitch at either side of both the drawstring channel openings and the turning gap.

8 Remove any pins or tacking and press the side seam open at each drawstring channel. Turn your work right sides out through the turning gap.

9 Make a line of small running stitches around each opening, catching the seam selvedge to ease the movement of the drawstrings later.

10 Turn the raw edges in at the turning gap and close by hand with a whip stitch.

6

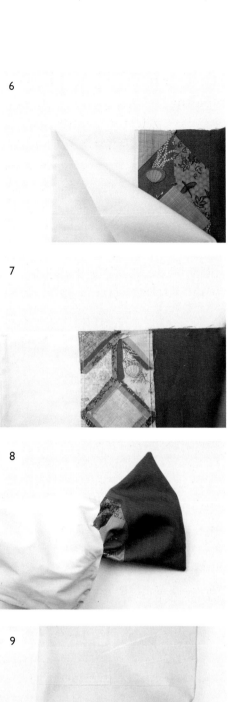

7

8

9

10

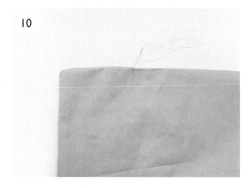

11 Push your lining down into your bag's outer, prodding the two bottom corners from the inside to make them as sharp as you can. Give your work a good press, ensuring the top edge where the outer meets the lining is sharp and crisp. Tack around the top edge, and twice again 1½in (3.8cm) and 2½in (6.3cm) below this (to form the drawstring channel). Use your machine to top stitch ⅛in (0.32cm) in from the top edge and again along both basted drawstring channels. Remove all tacking.

12 Fold one calico strip in half along its long axis and press with a hot iron. Use the machine to stitch a seam down the long edge and use the safety pin to turn it right side out. Press with a hot iron and repeat with the other strip to create two drawstrings.

13 Use the safety pin to run one drawstring through its channel, in from the right and all the way around and back out through the right. Do the same with the second drawstring, entering and exiting the channel from the left-hand side. Finish by simply knotting the two ends of each drawstring together to prevent them disappearing into the channel when in use.

11

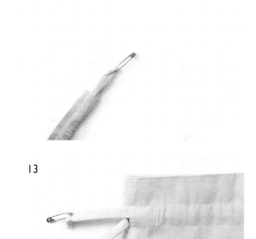

12

13

TEMPLATES

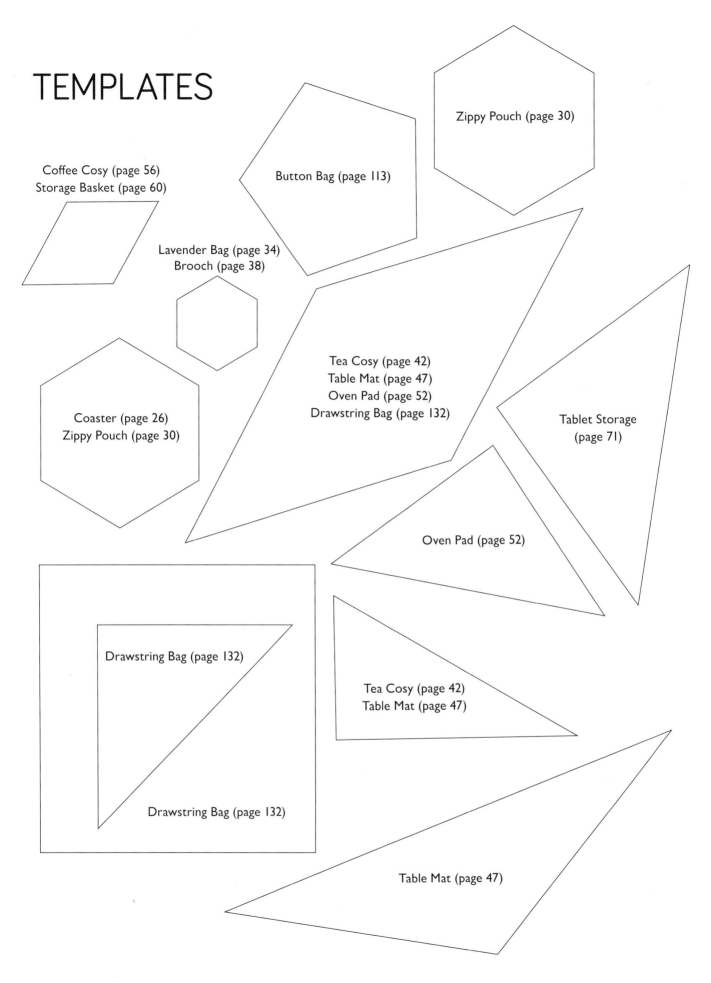

Coffee Cosy (page 56)
Storage Basket (page 60)

Button Bag (page 113)

Zippy Pouch (page 30)

Lavender Bag (page 34)
Brooch (page 38)

Tea Cosy (page 42)
Table Mat (page 47)
Oven Pad (page 52)
Drawstring Bag (page 132)

Tablet Storage
(page 71)

Coaster (page 26)
Zippy Pouch (page 30)

Oven Pad (page 52)

Drawstring Bag (page 132)

Tea Cosy (page 42)
Table Mat (page 47)

Drawstring Bag (page 132)

Table Mat (page 47)

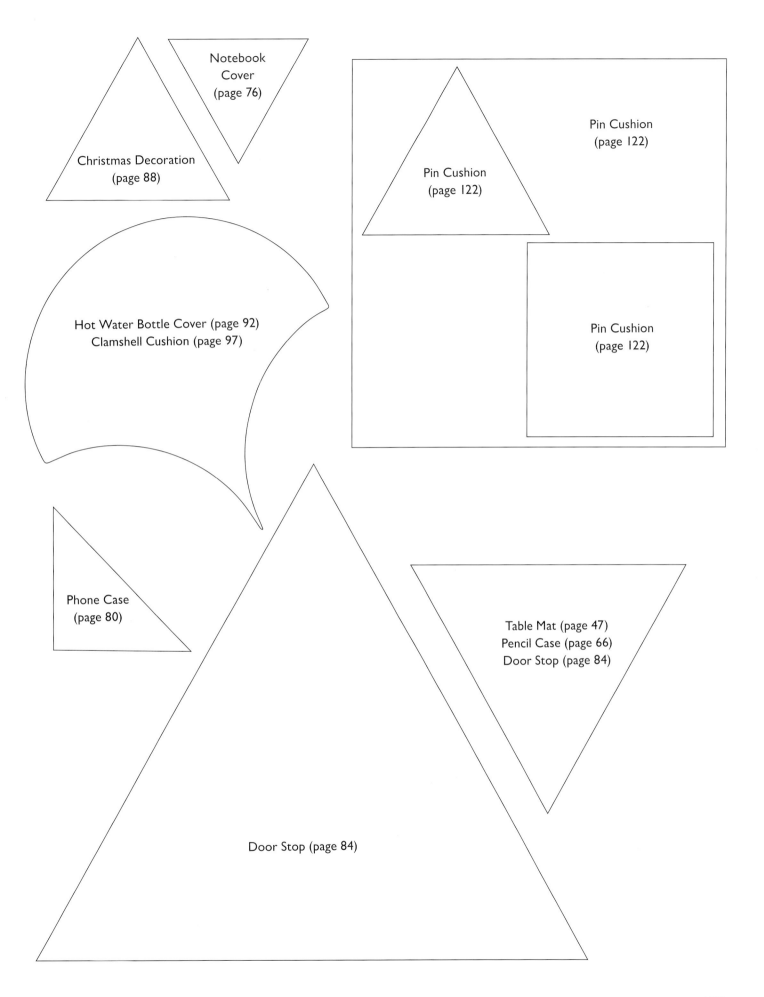

Notebook
Cover
(page 76)

Christmas Decoration
(page 88)

Pin Cushion
(page 122)

Pin Cushion
(page 122)

Pin Cushion
(page 122)

Hot Water Bottle Cover (page 92)
Clamshell Cushion (page 97)

Phone Case
(page 80)

Table Mat (page 47)
Pencil Case (page 66)
Door Stop (page 84)

Door Stop (page 84)

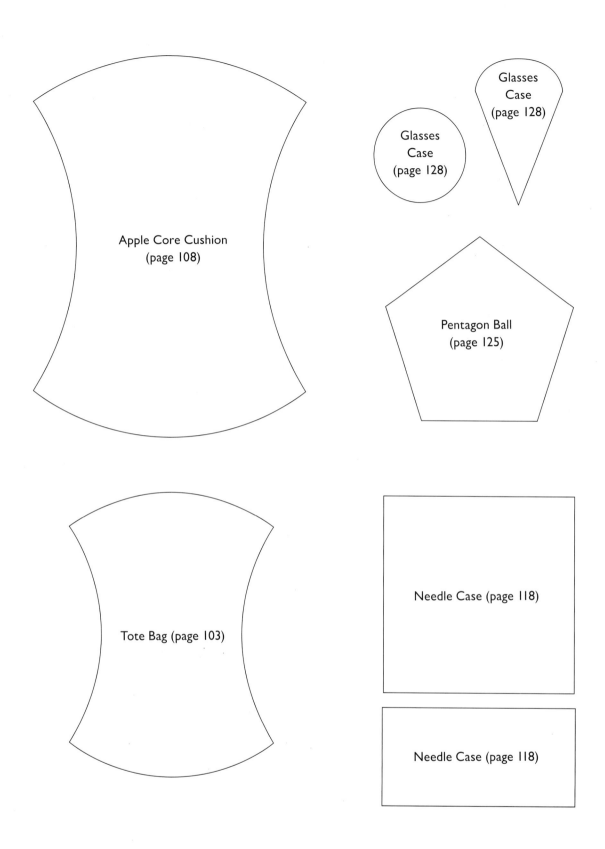

Apple Core Cushion
(page 108)

Glasses
Case
(page 128)

Glasses
Case
(page 128)

Pentagon Ball
(page 125)

Tote Bag (page 103)

Needle Case (page 118)

Needle Case (page 118)

Tea Cosy Quilting
Template
(enlarge by 200%)
(page 42)

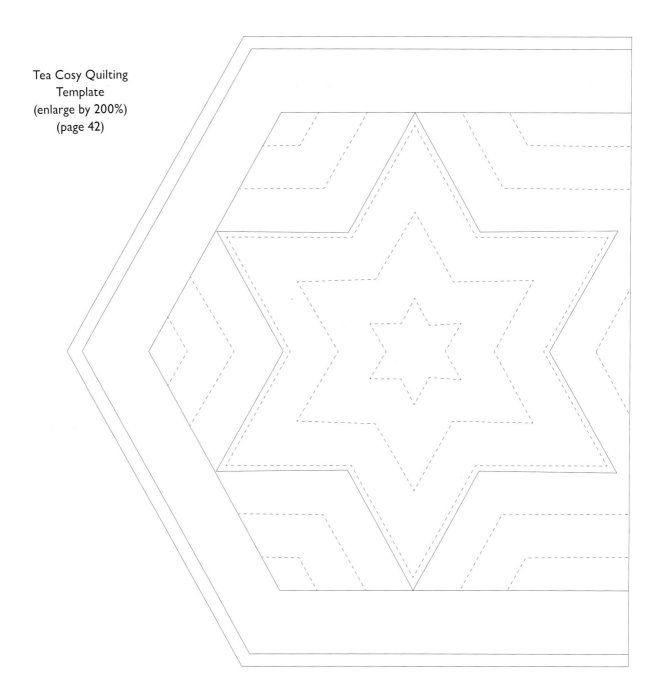

RESOURCES

English paper pieces
Sew & Quilt
www.sewandquilt.co.uk

Fabrics
Makower
www.makoweruk.com
Lady Sew and Sew
www.ladysewandsew.co.uk

Fusible interfacing
Just Between Friends
www.justbetweenfriends.co.uk

Fusible wadding (batting)
Plush Addict
www.plushaddict.co.uk

Interfacing
Vlieseline
www.vlieseline.com

Sewing machine
Bernina
www.bernina.com

Thread
Aurifil threads
www.aurifil.com

Wadding (batting)
Lady Sew and Sew
www.ladysewandsew.co.uk

ACKNOWLEDGEMENTS

I have so enjoyed designing, creating and writing the patterns for the projects in this book and am very grateful to everyone who played a part in the process. Many thanks to Darren and the team at Quail Studio for their hard work and great design. Thanks to Wendy Hobson for her meticulous technical editing and endless patience. To Makower, thank you for all the lovely fabrics to work with. Finally, thank you to my partner Alan who is so supportive with my fabric obsession.

Janet Goddard

With many thanks to everyone involved in the design and production of this book; those who contributed to the design, materials, photography and editing. A special thank you to my grandmother Nancy and mother Ann who taught me to sew and knit at a very early age, gifting me skills to enrich my life, and which I continue to develop and enjoy. Finally, with love to Harrison and Martha.

Jemima Schlee

To order GMC books, contact:

GMC Publications Ltd
Castle Place, 166 High Street,
Lewes, East Sussex,
BN7 1XU
United Kingdom
Tel: +44 (0)1273 488005
www.gmcbooks.com

INDEX